Read with
not need at
The again.

40p

'eople

RANCH

FP 87.

HAMPSHIRE COUNTY LIBRARY
WITHDRAWN

Building Your Business

Other titles in this series are:

Know Your Law
by Greville Janner QC MP

How to Win Profitable Business
by Tom Cannon

How to Manage Money
by D Donleavy and M Metcalfe

For details see back of book

How to Manage People

Ron Johnson

Business Books
London Melbourne Sydney Auckland Johannesburg

Business Books Ltd

An imprint of the Hutchinson Publishing Group

17-21 Conway Street, London W1P 6JD

Hutchinson Group (Australia) Pty Ltd
30-32 Cremorne Street, Richmond South, Victoria 3121
PO Box 151, Broadway, New South Wales 2007

Hutchinson Group (NZ) Ltd
32-34 View Road, PO Box 40-086, Glenfield, Auckland 10

Hutchinson Group (SA) (Pty) Ltd
PO Box 337, Bergvlei 2012, South Africa

First published 1984
© R M Johnson

Set in Megaron

Printed in Great Britain by The Anchor Press Ltd
and bound by Wm Brendon & Son Ltd
both of Tiptree, Essex

British Library Cataloguing in Publication Data
Johnson, Ron
How to manage people.
1. Personnel management
I. Title
658.3   HF5549

ISBN 0 09 151830 X (Cased)
0 09 151831 8 (Pbk)

Building Your Business

Series Editor: Tom Cannon

The last decade has witnessed a growing awareness of the importance of a healthy small business sector. The individuality, flexibility and creativity of the entrepreneur are recognized as vital to economic prosperity. Yet the same period has thrown up more and more challenges to the small firm. Competition has become more rigorous, while the need for efficiency and the effective application of resources has increased sharply. Perhaps the most valuable of these resources today is knowledge.

This series of books has been designed specifically for the entrepreneur, to bring to the owner and manager of the small firm vital areas of knowledge and information. The aim throughout has been to break down the barriers between theory and practice. The books are 'action-oriented' and this action-orientation is built into the texts themselves. Each book is broken down into self-contained Units. Each Unit sets out **Key Issues**, develops the issues and ends with **Action Guidelines**. Wherever possible, examples are drawn from the actual experience of small business people. Each author is an expert in his own field but equally at home with the application of his expertise to the small firm.

Growing recognition of the needs of the small firm has led to a range of initiatives to provide assistance. Government at a national and local level, large companies, banks and voluntary agencies are actively seeking ways to help the owner and manager of the small business to thrive. However the key characteristic of this type of company is its dependence on individual effort and skill. The onus for survival and prosperity lies on the man or woman who turns these ideas into action. This series focuses on the key areas of customers, money, people and the law. The ideas presented will help provide the management expertise which leads to success.

Contents

	Preface	11
	How to Use this Book	12
1	Your Firm and Your People	13
	Introduction	13
	Key people	14
	Positive motivation	18
	Relationships	19
	Action guidelines	21
2	People and Jobs	22
	Describing jobs	22
	Your own job	26
	Use of time	29
	Action guidelines	31
3	People Working Together	32
	Teamwork	32
	Improving teamwork	37
	Action guidelines	40
4	Where People Work	41
	Environment	41
	Security	46
	Action guidelines	48
5	Looking Ahead with People	49
	Problems of change	49
	Prepare for change	51
	Preparing for consultation	55
	Preparing for negotiating	56
	Action guidelines	61
6	How to Set Targets	62
	Target levels	62

	Practicalities	65
	Reviewing targets	66
	Action guidelines	70
7	**How to Encourage People**	71
	Why people come	71
	What discourages people	76
	What encourages people	77
	Action guidelines	81
8	**How to Correct People**	82
	Positive correction	82
	Reasons for mistakes	83
	Analysing mistakes	87
	Deliberate misbehaviour	90
	Action guidelines	92
9	**How to Talk and Listen**	93
	Two-way process	93
	Were you heard?	95
	Did you hear?	98
	People in groups and meetings	103
	Action guidelines	108
10	**How to Write to People**	109
	Clarity and style	109
	To whom?	111
	Why write?	112
	Choosing words	113
	Circulars	115
	Action guidelines	118
11	**The Opposite Sex**	119
	The difference	119
	Man in charge	120
	Woman in charge	121
	Discrimination	122
	Working together	123
	Action guidelines	125
12	**Coping with Young People**	126
	What's new?	126
	Positive help	128
	Building up confidence	131
	Timekeeping	132

	Relating to older workers	132
	Action guidelines	134
13	Employing Disabled People	135
	Loyal workers	135
	Filling a vacancy	136
	Equipment and premises	137
	Action guidelines	140
14	People and Technology	141
	Aspects of change	141
	Before deciding	142
	Knock-on effects	143
	Getting going	147
	Reviewing	148
	Action guidelines	149
15	Leadership	150
	Your management style	150
	Your motivation	151
	Flexibility	153
	Self-image	154
	Technical questions	155
	Decision-making	156
	Action guidelines	157
16	Hiring More People	158
	Another person	158
	Writing down the job	160
	Building up the person you want	163
	Ways of recruiting	164
	Dealing with applications	166
	Interviewing	166
	Job offer	169
	Action guidelines	170
17	Hiring a Specialist	171
	The need for a specialist	171
	Criteria for selection	172
	Recruitment	175
	Selection	177
	Job offer	178
	Discussing the job description	179
	Action guidelines	181

18 Hiring a Graduate — 182
Why a graduate? — 182
What you can offer — 183
What kind of graduate? — 185
The graduate arrives — 187
Keep in touch — 188
Action guidelines — 191

19 Helping the Newcomer — 192
The first day — 192
Training — 196
Flexibility — 198
Health and safety — 199
Action guidelines — 200

20 Retirement, Redundancy and Resignation — 201
Retirement — 201
Resignations — 202
Redundancy — 203
Action guidelines — 208

21 Helping People Improve — 209
Developing people — 209
Creative groups — 211
Skills for new tasks — 212
Who needs training? — 213
Keeping records — 216
Action guidelines — 218

20 Keeping Ahead with People — 219
The craft — 219
Key tasks — 220
Key people — 221
The future — 223

Appendix: The Way People Contribute to Meetings — 224

Index — 227

Preface

This book is not really about people in general. It is about you and your people. Unless you work alone on a desert island you will soon discover that success in your business depends, among other things, on how well you relate to people and gain their support for your endeavours. This is particularly true of the people who work for you. That's what this book is all about. Since it is about you and your people, it will never be finished unless you add flesh to the skeleton provided here.

Use ideas that seem appropriate to you. Set aside those which are irrelevant – but don't be too hasty. Some of these ideas may be worth a second look. Some people are born managers and some will probably never be much good at dealing with people. Most of us could be a whole lot better with a few insights and a little effort. If you want to try, read on.

I am grateful to Robin Williams and Meredith Belbin for helpful comments and discussions during the writing of this book and to Blue Stevens for her enthusiasm and patience in converting my scribble into typescript.

Ron Johnson

How to Use this Book

This book assumes that the reader wants to be a better manager. Frankly, reading a book will not help a great deal, but working through this book will. You can only learn to manage by actually managing. But your learning can be considerably improved if you begin to notice what is going on around you, how you are behaving and how people are responding to you.

This book tries to help you to become more aware of these things so that you can become more effective. At one level you can read through the book and pick up a few tips here and there, ignoring all the bits where you are asked to do some work. If you are not serious about being a manager, it might do you a little good – but not much.

If you really want to be a better manager, you should take the trouble to work through the exercises. They will not take a long time, but they will make you think, and what is much more important, most of them will make you think about your own firm and your own situation. If you fail to relate what is said in the book to your company, then most of your time and money spent on this book may be wasted.

Perhaps the best way to use the book is to read it all quickly, then to go back and work carefully through Units 1 to 15, then skip to Units 21 and 22. You should work through the appropriate Units in the section from 16–20 as the need arises.

It must be emphasized that this is not a book about the law, although in some places reference is made to legal aspects of employment where relevant. The reader should turn to other texts to ensure compliance with the many demands of the law in the employment field.

You will learn to manage better if you manage to learn at the same time!

1
Your Firm and Your People

- To a large extent success in your business depends on the way you deal with people.
- You can assess the strengths and weaknesses of the people who make a really critical contribution to the firm's fortunes.
- By working to improve the motivation and ability of the people who work for you, you can improve the effectiveness of your whole operation.

Introduction

If you employ someone, or if you work with a partner, then 'people' issues matter to you. If you intend to employ someone extra or to take on a partner, 'people' issues are absolutely crucial. If you employ so many people that you don't really know what they all do, then you have a real 'people' challenge.

Taking an interest in the people who work for and with you is a commercial necessity, not just a benevolent pastime. You should aim to be as good at dealing with people as you are at providing goods and/or services, and at managing cash. Your business can be ruined by poor people-management, or its fortunes enhanced by having your people right behind you, able to do their jobs well and ready to pull out all the stops.

This book is really only partly finished. It's intended to be about you, your firm and your people, so that only you can add the finishing touches by filling it out in the light of your own situation.

You will need to use the checklists at the end of each chapter and to make notes of any useful points as they apply to your own firm as you go along. Managing people is basically about relationships. It's about relationships between people for the most part, although financial and material resources play a big part and so does the way in which information gets around (or doesn't get around!). In essence you have relationships between these three factors to consider – your people, yourself and the material side of the firm (including information).

Key people

Let's make a start now. Get out the list of the people who work in your firm. How well do you know these people? How well do you rate their enthusiasm, their ability, their performance and their contribution to the success of the enterprise? In thinking about this be careful to distinguish enthusiasm from ability. Without both, people will not perform at their best. If you have more than 20 or 30 people working for you, you may not know very closely the work of all of them. In any case, to start with you may find it tedious to consider too many people. Select say five or six people who work for you and that you consider important to the success of the firm. Set down what you think of their performance. Use the performance checklist in Figure 1 if you find it helpful. You may also find it useful to draw up an 'organization chart' showing who is responsible for various jobs (see example in Figure 2).

If we look at the performance checklist for a minute you will notice the word 'seem' is used in **motivation** and **potential**. We can't really be sure about people's motivation or potential, but if we're in the business of managing people we need to make judgements – but be prepared to change our minds as new evidence comes along. As far as **ability** goes we can, of course, only see what the person does; he or she may be capable of far more, given the right conditions and encouragement. Making it possible for people to give of their best involves making a careful distinction between what people want to do, can do and might be able to do with training or under the right conditions. Your ideas about how well each individual gets on with other people may also be somewhat subjective, but it is worth thinking about.

Figure 1 *Performance checklist*

You may find it helpful to complete one of these forms for each of your key people.

NAME

JOB (explain briefly)

ATTRIBUTES

Motivation He or she:
- seems well motivated, always keen to do a good job   Score 2
- seems to do what's required and no more   Score 1
- seems poorly motivated, always needs encouragement or a push   Score 0

Ability He or she is:
- capable of doing the job well   Score 2
- just about able to cope with the job   Score 1
- not really able to do the job properly   Score 0

Potential He or she seems:
- able to improve and to be able to take on more responsibility in due course   Score 2
- able to improve ability to do the present job   Score 1
- at the limit of development: no further improvement in ability seems likely   Score 0

Relationships He or she seems:
- to get on well with others and to gain their co-operation   Score 2
- to barely get the level of co-operation required   Score 1
- to upset other people to the detriment of the work   Score 0

NOTE Do *not* add these figures up. Reflect upon what they mean for the business and what action you can take. See text.

Figure 2   *Simple organization chart*

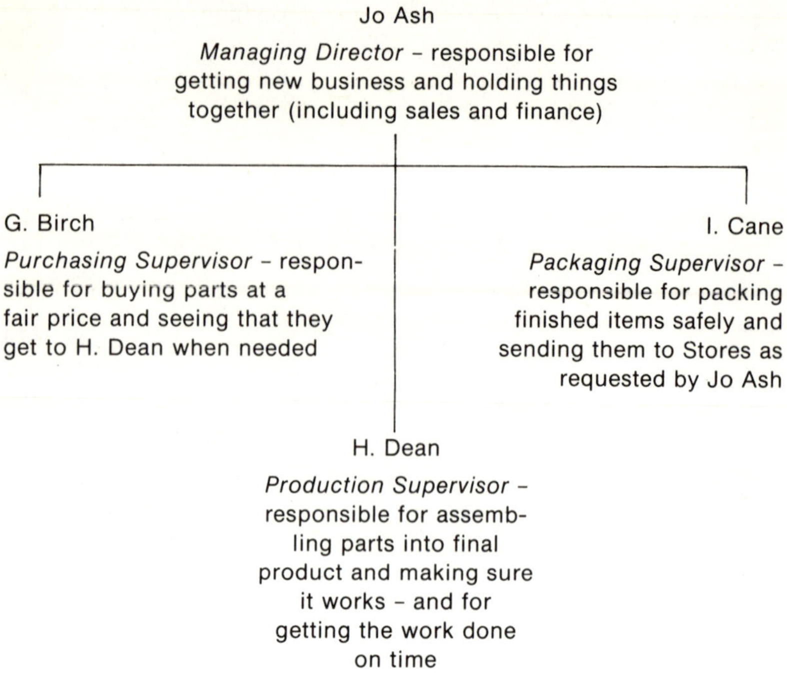

Jo Ash
Managing Director – responsible for getting new business and holding things together (including sales and finance)

G. Birch
Purchasing Supervisor – responsible for buying parts at a fair price and seeing that they get to H. Dean when needed

I. Cane
Packaging Supervisor – responsible for packing finished items safely and sending them to Stores as requested by Jo Ash

H. Dean
Production Supervisor – responsible for assembling parts into final product and making sure it works – and for getting the work done on time

Now if most of your people score zeros all along the line you are in real trouble. It's unlikely. You could, however, find that you have some people at the limit of their abilities – scoring 0 for P (Potential). But if they are reasonably well motivated (scoring 1 for M, Motivation) and just about able to do the job (scoring 1 for A, Ability), they may be quite satisfactory employees. Never despise those of humble ability who can stick at a job week in and week out, producing reasonable results. Some firms need these people. But they may not be the people to open up fresh markets or solve new problems. The time to be careful is when the demands of the job change:

- Will they be able to cope?
- Will they need help?
- Will you need to re-allocate responsibilities?

You may have someone who scores 0 for ability. In your opinion they are not really up to the job. What options do you have? You must decide first of all whether, with a little bit of help, this individual could learn to cope better. It may depend on the way the person is managed and you may find that all you have to do is to transfer the individual to work under someone else. There is no doubt that people are generally capable of more than we think at first sight. Changing the job, changing the boss, changing the tool or simply giving a bit of training, coaching and encouragement often makes for success. This approach is much better than thinking about dismissal – a very last resort, which in most cases implies managerial failure.

If you have someone who scores 0 for motivation – worse still if you have more than one scoring zero – this is a matter you must tackle as a matter of real urgency. You have the following problems to consider:

- First, what, if anything, is demotivating these people?
- Do they feel underpaid or undervalued?
- Are the working conditions depressing – a dingy room with dark paintwork, poor lighting, no outside window and little air? Don't underestimate the effects of adverse working conditions. They may not give rise to strident complaints, but they can be a reason for people failing to give of their best.
- Do they have all the tools they need, adequate space to work, access to information about exactly what is needed and the standards required?
- Are they feeling insecure, frightened of losing their jobs or being told off for lack of productivity? Psychological factors like this must be carefully considered by the person who is concerned about people at work.

If only one person scores 0 for motivation, then the cause is more likely to be personal. It could be a problem at work, or it could be something quite outside, e.g. family or financial worries. The boss can be sympathetic, but should not probe too deeply or try to act as an amateur psychiatrist. If it seems to be a personal health problem, the individual should be urged to obtain medical advice.

In the case of alcohol problems, the individual should be urged to seek proper help, and be supported by the firm if he or she makes a real effort to deal with it. This is not an easy matter to deal with and you should tread warily. You might make matters worse if you are not careful.

Positive motivation

So much for the negative side. Even when there are no problems of personal relationships, family worries, money worries, working conditions and so on, that still does not provide a positive force for being keen on getting results. We need to consider how to enthuse people with a desire to achieve results, to improve quality and increase production. If we are to be successful, we need to know more about people and how they become enthusiastic. If you start to take more notice of people, you can deduce quite a lot for yourself. Why not get out a sheet of paper, before you read on, and just jot down a number of answers to this question by completing the following sentence: '**I think people work with enthusiasm when . . .** '.

Have you got your list? You'll get much more out of the next section if you have spent a few minutes thinking about this. What did you come up with? You might have said, 'I think people work with enthusiasm when they get more money for working harder or producing more'. That's a fair answer, and its true for a lot of people – up to a point. But it really is not true for some people – is it? You might have finished your sentence: 'when they can see the results of their work'. That's a good point. Many people take much more interest in their work when they see how it fits into an overall picture, or when they can make a complete article or component and see it as their own work. Unfortunately some jobs don't lend themselves to this, but where they do, it's an approach that's well worthwhile.

Being part of a team   You might have said: 'when they feel part of a team that is successful'. That's true for very many people. Do your people feel part of a team? Do they feel involved in a joint endeavour? Another possible answer might be: 'when their work is recognized by others'. A little encouragement and praise, if it's sincere, goes a long way. There are a number of rewards, like being informed – or better still consulted – about what's going on and what might develop in the future. Getting people to think about ways of making things better is a great way to stimulate enthusiasm. But beware. If you don't intend to take any notice of what people say, don't ask their advice. You'll soon be found out. People don't take kindly to hypocrites or to being patronized. If you ask people for their views and ideas, learn to listen and respond. If you can't use an idea, explain why. Do not just let it drop – or you will not get any more ideas and any enthusiasm you have generated will soon evaporate.

Another aspect of praise is simply to comment when a particular job has been done well or when a day has gone smoothly and fruitfully. But beware of doing this mechanically, or to a formula. If you spend some time each day or week simply noticing what goes on, you will probably conclude that when the chips are down you depend a great deal on your people. Don't manage them by inventing or adopting a set of rules like a computer. Recognize that each person is different. There are a lot of similarities, but they pale into insignificance beside the individuality we see, especially in the smaller firm. Not only is one person different from another, but each person is different from time to time. His or her ability or motivation will change with circumstances. Individuals often have complex personalities, adopting different roles at different times. The quiet worker who does what he is told may be a leading light in the local darts club, and if you mention the word 'pigeon' you may find he has a wealth of knowledge and enthusiasm you never dreamt about. In contrast there are some individuals who have such pronounced characteristics that they nearly always behave in much the same way.

Relationships

In many ways the section on relationships with people does not quite fit the same pattern as the other three items, but it is of crucial importance. You may find that one of your employees is so bad at relating to other people that it seriously affects efficiency in the job. You may also have problems if another gets on too well with people, i.e. spending all day chatting rather than getting on with the job.

So get to know your people, what discourages them, what makes them enthusiastic.

Having looked at the strengths and weaknesses of your people, you ought to have a look at your own capabilities. Then you can consider how to overcome weaknesses and build on strengths so that you and your people can build a better company.

The rest of this book is devoted to different aspects of these issues and to specific problems and challenges faced by managers in their everyday experiences. Some Units may not be important to you at the moment. Just skim through them and move on. You can come back to them later when it makes sense to you.

Action Guidelines

1 Have you got a chart of your key people and their jobs?

2 Have you considered each of your key people and how you can help them to do a better job, e.g.
   (a) working conditions;
   (b) tools and equipment;
   (c) information;
   (d) training;
   (e) coaching?

3 Have you considered each of your key people and what you can do to help and encourage them to improve, e.g.
   (a) payment systems;
   (b) complete components;
   (c) teamwork;
   (d) praise;
   (e) consultation?

2
People and Jobs

- A few minutes spent in writing down the essence of people's jobs and discussing them can prove most useful.
- Factors like deadlines, health and safety and new challenges must be taken into account.
- A critical look at your own job can lead to very real improvements in the way the firm is run.
- Time, especially your time, is very valuable: see that you make good use of it.

Describing jobs

Just think again about the half-dozen or so people you consider important in your business. Perhaps you wrote down a few things about them as individuals as you read Unit 1. Now let's think about the jobs they are doing. People study jobs more closely for a variety of reasons, e.g. for fixing wage levels and status, for selecting newcomers, hopefully able to perform well in the particular situation, to improve efficiency in the organization or to decide on what training to give to the people concerned. If you are mainly concerned about status and payments (or other rewards) you will probably use a 'job evaluation' approach. This can be useful, especially in middle-sized and larger firms, but is by no means as simple and 'scientific' as it sounds. Job evaluation methods are essentially ways of sorting out people's opinions of what various aspects of a job are worth and using that as a basis for determining wages, status and rewards. As these methods are based on opinions, you can see there is plenty of room for endless disputes and, what's worse, for obviously wrong answers to come out of the process. These 'wrong' decisions can be difficult to change if the whole system is enmeshed in agreements with trade unions. Job evaluation is a useful and necessary tool, but you really need expert help to make it work properly. We will take another look later on.

When we want to improve performance rather than set reward levels, we use different kinds of tools. The commonest approach is to prepare a written description of the job, the so-called 'job description' (see Figures 3 and 4). There are a number of ways of doing this. A simple approach will be given here and there are more sophisticated methods if you consider the investment of time and money worthwhile. Some investment of time on your part in drawing up job descriptions for your key people – those who work directly for you – will almost certainly pay off. The thing to bear in mind is that it is in the work involved in drawing up the job description that the real value lies, rather than in the written document. This is where you can find out ways to help your key people

Figure 3 *Simple job description*

NAME:

JOB TITLE:

JOBHOLDER REPORTS TO:

PEOPLE REPORTING TO JOBHOLDER:

MAIN RESPONSIBILITIES: *(Keep these as few as you can and each one described in as few words as possible. Don't bother with sentences. Short notes will do.)*

Figure 4 *Possible additions to job description*

MAIN RESULT AREAS:

TARGET DATES:

KEY CONTACTS:

to be more effective. If you get someone else to draw it up, you have in effect thrown away most of the value of the exercise. The other person who must be closely involved is, obviously, the jobholder.

It's a good idea for the jobholder and the jobholder's boss (you in this case!) each to jot down the points that seem most important. Then the two of you can get together and compare notes. Hopefully each of you will have written down the same things, though perhaps in different words and with different emphases. The most interesting parts are these differences in emphasis between you and the jobholder on specific topics.

There may be items you write down and not the jobholder – or vice-versa. This may be simply an oversight, but that's unlikely to be the whole explanation. An oversight in an important area probably means that for some reason you – or the jobholder – don't regard this as really important. It may be fruitful to think about whether this is true and, if so, why. Coming now to the outright gaps, these may represent significant differences in view about what the job really entails. If this comes as a surprise to you, such differences of view mean that you and the jobholder have not been getting through to each other, or to use the current jargon, you have not been communicating effectively with each other. We shall return to this topic in Unit 9.

There's every probability that if you straighten out these discrepancies, the working relationships between you and your key people will improve significantly and your firm will be more successful as a result. But don't push things too far. The law of diminishing returns operates here just as it does in most aspects of the business. A little ambiguity here and there helps the wheels go round. If everyone has a clearly defined job you're in dead trouble as soon as something comes up that isn't in anybody's job description. Leave an escape clause in like: 'Your job includes doing anything reasonable that I ask you for the good of the business'. Keep the number of words you use down to the absolute minimum.

There are many jobs where this simple procedure will give you all you need. This is particularly true of routine jobs where work flows evenly through the paint shop, the assembly line or the office.

There are three important exceptions:

- Jobs where there are occasional crises or deadlines to be met.
- Jobs where there are significant risks to health and safety.
- Jobs where the work is constantly varied and changing.

Deadlines and safety For jobs with crises or deadlines it is worth taking a closer look at a few of these events in turn – soon after each one has taken place – and trying to disentangle who did what, and in particular who took some of the key decisions. Half an hour or so spent discussing this with two or three of your colleagues involved may well reveal that some of the decisions are taken by people who are not well equipped to do so, or that some of the ways in which you get results could be improved. It also helps you to write better notes on the job description!

All jobs have some element of danger, however remote it may seem. One can have a nasty accident in an office or shop, and there is the ever-present risk of fire. Simple precautions – keeping drawers closed and regular fire drills and inspection of fire doors and appliances – should be the order of the day. Where appropriate a note should be made in the job description of the person responsible.

Some jobs, however, have more imminent or dramatic dangers, and escape or accident drills and so forth may be most important. Again this should be a matter for discussion in drawing up the job description, and noted on the form. In such matters it is important that you, yourself, recognize the value and need for safe working practices in a commercial sense as well as for humanitarian reasons. Then when you come to discuss them with your people they will sense your concern and respond. If you are offhand about safety, they will be too.

Safety of customers A somewhat similar problem concerns the safety of your customers. If you are a food manufacturer or purveyor of foodstuffs you must carefully observe the rules for handling and storing foods – otherwise you run the risk of giving someone food poisoning. That's not good for business. The same kind of thing applies when you are making potentially dangerous products like electrical goods. Your concern for the safety of your customers must be real and genuine – and communicated to your people. It's simply not good enough to tell your staff the proper way to handle food or to make safe products. If they perform such operations without understanding or being convinced of the importance of safe procedures, the day will come when they will cut corners and take risks – which could lead to serious damage to your business. By all means put this in the job description – but don't rely on that slip of paper alone. You need to create as it were a total 'culture' of concern for safety and health in your outfit.

Varied and changing jobs Now let's consider the third problem – a job that's one long succession of new challenges. That is characteristic of many management jobs – and probably true of your own working life. The methods I shall describe below should, therefore, be applied to your own job and that of any other people in your firm who have management-type responsibilities. The most important approach is to look for key results, and this can usefully be backed up by an occasional 'diary analysis' – see below. **Incidentally, getting your own job straight is an important as other people's if you want an effective working team, so don't dismiss your own job description as irrelevant.**

Your own job

The trouble with being in charge is that you can do what you like, when you like and how you like. In one sense that's a great asset, but the danger is that doing what you enjoy all the time will not make the firm successful. To do that you'll have to spend time doing some of the jobs you don't enjoy very much, or make sure that someone else does them – and does them properly. I assume you have a business plan and know roughly what profit, turnover and cash flow you are working towards over the next twelve months or so. If you have not got that or something like it which is appropriate to your business then you are unlikely to manage your people well. Get that done. Buy another book or go to classes and get this sorted out quickly. You must master the discipline of costing, estimating and financial control at the outset.

If you have a business plan:

- Look for the elements that make for success: key delivery dates to keep customers happy, prompt issue of invoices to keep the cash flowing, effectively timed sales promotion activities to keep the orders coming along.
- List the areas where results are really vital to your success.
- Look at those key factors and dates in relation to your workload and see if you can set monthly targets for yourself – and perhaps for your key staff.

As you look at these issues you will probably come to realize that, apart from the key people in your firm, there are a number of key contacts outside. These are people with whom you want to keep in touch, so that if you need their help at a difficult time you can quickly get in touch and expect co-operation. It may be the purchasing managers for three or four of your major clients or the despatch manager at one of your important suppliers. Make a careful note of these people (use Figures 5 and 6 if you find it helpful). Now make out a job description for yourself using Figure 4 as well as Figure 3. Once you've done that, you might show it to your right-hand man (or woman) in the firm and see whether they agree with your conclusions. You may find such a chat well worth the investment of half an hour of your time. Try to do it away from the pressures of your office.

Figure 5 *Key people: chart for the boss*

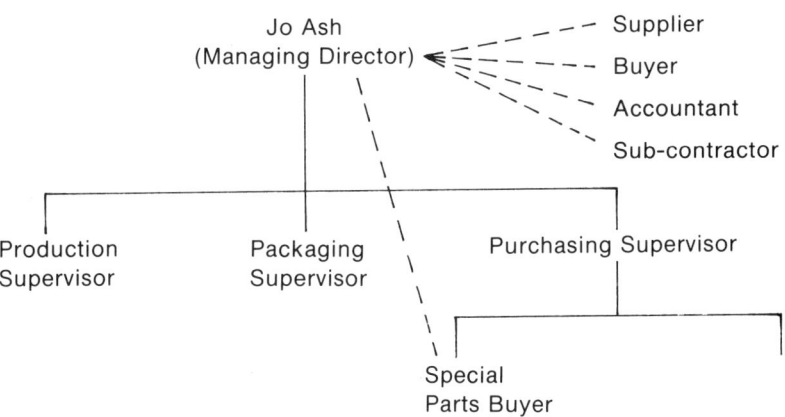

Figure 6 *Key contacts*

Your name:	Why are they important to you in terms of achieving your objectives?	How often do you think you should speak with them – and why?
People who report to you:		
People who report to the people who report to you – but with whom you wish to keep in touch:		
People outside the firm who are important to the success of your enterprise:		
NOTE: Don't forget your accountant and the bank manager. Should they be included?		

Use of time

A further check you can now undertake is the 'diary analysis'. If you keep a detailed diary of how you really spend your time – not how you hoped to spend it – you can do a simple analysis using that. Go through a typical week listing (say to the nearest 15 minutes) how you spent your time, with whom and why. Then try to make a statement about how useful that was – especially in relation to your main result areas, your target dates and your key contacts. Frankly, it is most unlikely that your existing diary will be of any use at all in this exercise, so you will have to do a chore. It will take a little time and discipline, but you could find the results valuable.

- Rule up a few sheets of paper as in Figure 7.
- Choose a reasonably typical period and keep a log for the entire working week – in and out of the office.
- Be careful to record interruptions and how long they take. At this stage do not concern yourself with the 'Comment' column. Just make sure you have the information written down.

Soon after you have completed the week's diary, sit down quietly and think about each activity. Write in the 'Comment' column what you think you achieved. Don't linger too long over each item; this is not a scientific study. You are just trying to get the feel of how well

Figure 7   *Diary analysis*

Date	Time	Activity	Duration	Comment

you use your time and expertise in relation to your objectives, main result areas and key contacts.

If you do this diary work carefully you will probably find that you spent a lot of time doing things that someone else in the firm – whose time is less valuable than your own – could have done. You may find yourself doing things you like rather than things which help forward the business. You may find, to your horror, that some important items were overlooked or deferred because of your preoccupation with less important matters. The diary work will not solve any of these things, but it will help you to see them more clearly and to know what action you must take to improve your own efficiency. It will almost certainly give you new insights into your own job and what it entails, and you may need to revise your own job description.

If you find this diary work useful, you can commend it to some of your senior colleagues. If you feel that you or some of your senior colleagues could make better use of your time, an investment of a couple of days and a few hundred pounds on a course is likely to be a sound investment. Many managers find they can save an hour or two a week. But the more important benefit is the greater clarity with which you can see the job and what needs to be done to achieve results. **Don't forget that your time and that of your key people is an extremely valuable resource.**

One way or another you can thus get people to understand more clearly what their jobs entail and what really matters. It's useful to write a few words on a sheet of paper – a job description. But don't get bogged down in paperwork. Always remember that it is the discussion that leads up to the bit of paper that matters, and after that the occasional chat to see how things are going. We will come back to this in Units 5 and 6.

Action Guidelines

1 Have you got a clear idea of your own job, the main result areas, the target dates and the key people involved?

2 Have you had a chat with each of the people who report to you about their jobs?

3 Have you got a sheet of paper for each person which summarizes the key points about the job – a job description?

4 Have you considered looking at some critical events to see what you can learn from them?

5 Have you considered the health and safety aspects of these jobs, and any other sporadic but important features?

6 Have you considered keeping a special diary for a week to see what you can learn from your own activities?

7 Have you considered using this special diary idea for some of your key people?

3
People Working Together

- In most firms success depends on a group of people working effectively together.
- A spirit of teamwork has to be created and maintained by conscious effort.
- Understanding between team members, people communicating with each other and sharing goals are important.
- Reactions to a crisis give a good indication of the health of the team.
- There are a number of steps you can take to improve teamwork in your outfit.

Teamwork

It is quite possible for a group of people in an organization to work with a high degree of individuality and independence. Each person can do his or her own 'thing', just occasionally interacting with other people in the firm by a telephone call, passing across a memorandum or whatever. Indeed there are some small organizations where a gaggle of prima-donnas, with secretarial back-up, may provide quite a good service. Even in cases like this, however, it is quite easy for misunderstandings to arise inadvertently – or perhaps sometimes deliberately – which impede the business. The ability of a group of people to pull together, to help each other out and to understand each other well is, more often than not, essential for a small organization to be effective. Sometimes this situation can be achieved without conscious effort on the part of the boss. His own personality and the nature of the work, the room in which they operate and so forth can attract the kind of people and provide the environment that encourages team spirit and teamwork. If you have this you are fortunate. You may not have an urgent need to read the rest of the chapter, but just before you turn over to Unit 4, make sure you keep this team working well together. Better spend a few minutes reading this Unit so that you understand what is going on and how you can encourage good work practices to continue. There is another point to consider. If the group is *too* chatty and cosy that may not, after all, be good for the firm. Getting the balance right is hard enough in many cases; keeping it can be even harder.

Most likely there is a small group of people in your enterprise who really make the difference between success or failure.

- Do they work as a team – or just as individuals?
- Do they keep things back, blame each other when things go wrong?

Spend a few minutes completing the questions in Figure 8. There's nothing clever or precise about these questions. They are just to help you think about teamwork. If your team scores ten out of ten, you have no worries at the moment. But read on, you will want to know how to keep up this high score.

Communication The first question is about communication. Many organizations don't spend enough time thinking about how to make sure people know what they need to work well together. Often individuals don't know enough about the other person's job in the team:

- What are his goals?
- How does he or she measure success?
- What does she need to get from me to do her job properly – and why?

The trouble is, if we set up a system for getting information moving around an organization but don't tell people who needs it and why,

Figure 8 *Teamwork rating*

Consider the group of people who – apart from you, the boss – really run your outfit. Think of them as a team and rate their performance on the scale below. Circle the number that most closely represents the situation as you see it.

1 Team members always know enough about what is going on to play their parts effectively	2 1 0	Team members don't know enough about what is going on and often take inappropriate decisions
2 When problems arise, team members are quick to tell their colleagues and to work constructively together towards a solution	2 1 0	When problems arise, people try to solve them without reference to other team members
3 When things go wrong, team members work together to sort them out and to devise ways to prevent a recurrence	2 1 0	When things go wrong, team members spend more time and energy blaming each other than trying to make improvements and to prevent a recurrence
4 When someone is away, team members know each other so well that they can take decisions that are likely to fit in with the absent member's ideas	2 1 0	When someone is away, the team becomes paralysed because they are not sure how the absent member would take decisions
5 When new ideas are needed, every team member feels free to play his part in a constructive way	2 1 0	When new ideas are needed, team members are hesitant to say things that others would criticize

Remember that other members of the team may answer these questions differently.

it gradually assumes a low priority and is regarded as an imposition and a nuisance. When the pressure is on, the information flow dries up – just when it is needed most. This is why it is important to demand the minimum information flow – and expect more in practice. To get people to communicate effectively, they need to understand each other's role and in effect to do an implicit deal where one helps the other. This helps to build trust. Lack of trust is mostly the result of fear (of being taken for a ride) based on misunderstanding. (Of course some people cannot – it seems – be trusted, and they are difficult to work with.)

Attitudes to problem-solving The second question deals with attitudes to problem-solving, and again these attitudes are affected profoundly by questions of trust and understanding. People do not share problems with others if they think the others are likely to take selfish advantage of the situation. If each person is out for himself, rather than for the success of the team, problems will be hidden away rather than opened up and resolved. This brings in two very important issues – common goals and the basis of rewards.

If each team member sees himself simply achieving personal goals he is likely to be poor at helping out others except when it clearly suits his purpose. If on the other hand, he has worked with the team to determine *shared* goals, he will be very concerned to help another member. This needs to be reflected in the recognition and rewards. People cannot be expected to work together as a team unless they are recognized and rewarded for this. If you reward them for individual performance without regard to how the others are doing, don't be surprised if the team becomes divided and discussions become unconstructive or even destructive. Which brings us to the third question.

Coping with crises How a team copes with a disaster of some kind tells you a lot about them:

- Do they hang together, or look for one of their number to hang on his own!
- Do they work together to find ways to overcome the setback, or throw up their hands and look for someone to blame?

- Do they take the failure apart to see how they could prevent it happening again?
- Do they quickly conclude that it was the result of an individual's bad decision and that the individual should be censured, sacked or demoted?

Of course, if one member of your team is incompetent you have a problem: you have to decide whether the team can and should 'carry' that individual, or whether he or she should be replaced: this need not mean sacking the individual, but perhaps moving him or her to another job in the organization.

A disaster can be a fruitful source of learning, and a springboard for future improvements, or it can be a disheartening episode that simply pulls the enterprise down. The difference will depend to a large extent on whether you have a sound team. Your own behaviour, as the boss, will have an immediate effect. Your leadership during a disaster will be crucial.

Decision-making for absentees If we assume you have a group of people who each play their parts well, what happens when one is away for a time – as in Question 4? The critical length of time will vary from one firm to another, according to the time cycle or rate of turnover of business and therefore the speed with which decisions have to be made. In the old Covent Garden Vegetable Market, so full of interest and atmosphere, many decisions had to be made every day about the buying and selling prices of a variety of fruits and vegetables. There are many firms where important decisions can take a couple of weeks or more. Your business has its own time factors. If the team members know each other well enough – in a working sense, not socially – they will be able to take decisions reasonably in line with the absent member's way of working. If they don't know him or her that well they have two choices. They can take decisions and hope for the best or they can delay decisions as long as they can. Not very satisfactory, since the individual will have to live with some of the decisions of the first kind, and delay could cost money. There is another option – they could take decisions which make life easier for themselves to the absent member's disadvantage. Of course, what often happens is that the decisions are pushed up or down, to the boss or to the absent person's subordinate – if there is one. In the short run that will work, but the more an absentee's work can be shared by a small team the more effective the organization will be. If one person has to carry all the extra burden in addition to his or her own job, the business is likely to suffer.

New ideas If you run a simple, stable, repetitive operation, then Question 5 may not mean much to you. Most small outfits, however, are frequently confronted with new decisions about what products they should offer and to whom, where they should get supplies from, what equipment they should use, should it be leased or purchased and so on. Quite often it is clear that one member of the team has to make the decision. But the question is, to what extent should he talk it over with the others? How free will they be to chip in with ideas, suggestions and so forth? In a good team, members will feel free to raise such issues in discussion and to make their points without trying to score off each other.

Improving teamwork

So far we have been doing a kind of diagnosis and assessment on your team. Suppose, now you want to improve the team's performance in communication and mutual support. How can you set about it? That depends to some extent on how bad the problem is at present. If your team score is below six, you may find it necessary to have some meetings with the group to face up to the problems and to try to get agreement on how to improve. You can't actually force them to be better, but experience shows that if you go about it the right way most people would really like to work purposefully together.

If you decide to confront this issue together with your group, get Figure 8 copied and ask each of them to answer it. Then bring the group together and present the results (on a flip-chart or on a sheet given to each person). Then discuss some or all of the following issues.

Would we be more effective as a working group if we:

- Understood each other's jobs better?

- Understood the group's objectives better, and how we can work together to achieve them?
- Were more prepared to discuss problems that arise?
- Worked together on important business decisions, even when they seem to concern only one member?

If you can get a 'yes' to any of these questions or similar ones, you can determine which chime in more readily with your business needs. You have made a good start. The next critical step is to ask the group if they consider this important enough to spend a little time on it. If you can get a 'yes' to that, you are making good progress. To maintain momentum you must work on issues that concern everybody in the group. Don't focus on an issue that concerns two members, but seems remote from the interests of the others. Before the end of the first or second meeting, try to identify a topic of general interest, and where people agree that improvement would help. If you can't readily identify a problem to work on, here are one or two ideas. You will remember how you wrote down job descriptions in Unit 2. Now try to get the group to work together on a group task description. You might start by asking the group to discuss and complete the following sentence:

'Our business is. . . .'

Then you could move on to think about the key factors that make for success (reasonably priced raw materials delivered on time, good quality products, careful pricing, spotting quickly changes in demand, controlling cash flow, etc.). Don't feed in solutions, get the group to do the work. This is one way to start the group thinking about the total picture and how their efforts dovetail to make the firm successful. You can build on this by getting the group, on another occasion, to think about the key contacts outside, the people who control your supplies and accept your goods or services. In your business there may be officials in local or national government departments with whom you need to keep in touch, or officers of trade federations and suchlike. You could discuss why the firm needs the collaboration of these people and what these key individuals require from you.

As the group thinks about these demands and constraints they may be directed to think about how, collectively, they can plan to meet them. Get them to discuss how each individual and section of the business is involved and what role has to be fulfilled to make the firm successful.

This form of team-building is not easy if you have a poor team spirit to start with, and you may find it advisable to get some advice.

If the team is working reasonably well, but needs to improve, you can get into effective team-building without the need for an initial confrontation meeting. Simply call the folk together and seek their collective help in making progress in specific areas, or in planning, or in solving some problems. If you demonstrate that you are interested in what each person has to contribute in terms of work and ideas, team-building will start up spontaneously. As the group members hear each other making useful contributions in your meetings, they will be more prepared to communicate and collaborate with each other outside. As they see you value co-operation, they will co-operate.

Once again, you see, **the key factor in producing a good team is the boss - you!** In a later Unit we will consider how you can take stock of your own management style and how you can be more effective.

Action Guidelines

1 What sort of team have you got? What sort of team do you need?

2 What can you do to build up a sense of teamwork?

3 In what ways do you communicate with your people? How well do they communicate with each other?

4 How do you and your team react when sudden and serious problems arise?

4
Where People Work

- There is no doubt that where people work has a very real effect on how well they do their jobs. It can also affect their safety and morale.
- Check out safety and the efficiency of your premises at the same time.
- Do not overlook noise and light, and be especially careful how you use space.

Environment

The kind of place you provide for your people to work in, and its location, will influence what sort of people will work for you and how keen they will be to do a decent job. In many cases it will also affect how well they are able to do the job. Just now you may not be able to do very much about where your work premises are situated, or the state of decoration, layout of machinery and so forth. Nevertheless you should read through the Unit to see if there are some relatively inexpensive and minor changes you can make to improve the safety, morale and effectiveness of your people.

When you are about to embark on a move, or a rearrangement of the office or factory, or to spend some money improving the decor, you may find it helpful to read this Unit again and to work systematically through the checklist. At the planning stage there are items you can incorporate inexpensively, whereas to introduce them later can be costly.

Safety One factor you can never overlook is safety, and you must also ensure that you comply with all the legal side. If you employ people, you will need to comply with legislation and regulations concerning standards of heating and lighting, provision of washing and toilet facilities, health and safety provisions and so forth. These are well documented and you must comply with the rules currently in force (see Note at end of Unit). Don't forget to take out the proper insurance against liability for any bodily injury or disease sustained by one of your employees whilst working for you. You should also insure against injuries to visitors.

In this book it is not appropriate to enter into detailed consideration of specially hazardous situations like laboratories, mines and factory workshops, or with the special precautions needed to deal with nuclear materials, biological matter or hazardous chemicals. If this is the nature of your business you must consult appropriate experts or texts and make sure you take every reasonable precaution – for protecting the public as well as yourself and your people. In almost every case cleanliness, orderliness and the close observance of safe working practices are fundamental. Your own example and that of your senior staff are absolutely imperative. If you are sloppy, or fail to replace guards and to wear protective clothing as appropriate, do not be surprised if your people follow suit. If that leads to an accident, you will share the blame for it.

Periodically it is worth checking any elements of danger in your factory, shop or office, and ensuring that sensible precautions are taken. Do not neglect the office, for accidents can happen there as well as in the more obviously dangerous places. Office workers have fallen down stairs, hit their knees on protruding drawers, caught their fingers in guillotines and have been electrocuted.

Layout The layout of the factory, office or shop should be viewed critically from the viewpoint of efficiency and safety together. So often these are seen as opposing ideas, whereas in most cases an efficiently laid-out workplace is safer, and vice-versa. More accidents are caused by people falling over, bumping into objects or stepping on things than by the machinery itself.

This mean that particular attention should be paid to the condition of floors and stairs, obstructions in corridors, swing doors (which should have vision panels), the siting of furniture and machinery (especially if it has sharp corners and edges), trailing telephone wires and electrical leads, protruding drawers of desks and filing cabinets (which can tip over sometimes if two drawers are open at once), and adequate means of reaching high objects (step ladders and step stools).

There is also that rare event, but ever-present danger – fire. It should not take long to check out possible sources of fire – faulty electrical connections or apparatus, oil heaters and radiant electric fires, inflammable liquids, gas appliances and so forth. Suppose a fire did start:

- What would your staff do? (It is your job to see that they know what to do.)
- Do they know the escape routes? (Are you sure these are open or openable quickly when your people are at work?)
- Do they know how to set off the alarm and to call the fire brigade?
- Can they all hear the alarm if it does go off?
- Are you sure it works?
- What about disabled staff?
- Can they get out in an emergency?
- Do your people know how to use the fire fighting equipment and where it is?
- Do they know when to use it, and when to get out and close doors behind them?

If you have a number of people working in a building, you should have a fire drill from time to time to make sure they can all hear the alarm and know how to get out quickly and where to assemble for roll call.

You should take particular care over electrical and mechanical equipment. Loose connections, broken plugs and trailing leads are all potential sources of electrical shocks or fires. Moving machinery and especially moving blades are obvious sources of injury.

A less obvious, but very important source of accidents, especially back injuries, is the way people lift loads and move objects. Where lifting equipment is provided, people should be trained and encouraged to use it properly. There are, however, frequent occasions when people are expected to lift cartons of paper, cans of food or whatever. Train them to bend the legs and keep their backs straight, lifting from a low position. This may sound trivial, but it is in fact very important indeed. Many working days are lost through back strain.

Space and light It is pretty obvious that you will need a reasonable system for heating and ventilating the places where your people work. You can't expect decent work from people who are too hot, or too cold, or who are sitting in a draught. Lighting is also important. Make sure that people have light where it is needed. An overall system of lighting may not be enough if people have close work to do. Remember that most people like to be able to look out of a window and to work in daylight. It is not so much the view they need, so much as the feeling that they are not cut off from the outside. Of course, if you are running a mine or have workshops in the basement, you can't have a window. Even below ground, however, a 'window-effect' decor helps to improve the ambience – for example in a canteen.

The need for daylight seems to be particularly important when people's workloads can be sporadic, e.g. a receptionist. If your premises are above ground you will often find it possible to arrange the workspace so that your people can see the windows, and use the corners and blank walls for storage and toilet areas. Don't underestimate the effect of this on the morale and efficiency of your staff.

Noise and tidiness Questions of noise, dirt and tidiness are also important. Some jobs are inherently dirty, but it is surprising how clean and tidy you can keep workplaces with very little effort. Generally speaking if you clean as you go, the resulting improvement in efficiency offsets the cost of the time spent. Of course, there are some operations where the sensible time to clean up is after a shift or a production run. If you have a dirty, noisy and untidy place, the likelihood is that only noisy, untidy people will want to work there! Think about it. Do you think that will make good business sense?

The question of noise is not just a nuisance, it can be a very real health hazard. Fortunately much of the modern machinery is qiueter than the older versions. There are ways of mounting machinery (even typewriters!) that reduce the noise output. If the noise is really unavoidable, then you and your staff must use ear-muffs. You must not succumb to the idea that it is silly or undignified to wear them. It is silly to risk partial deafness – and that will be the result of exposure to excessive noise. Even noise well below danger levels can be distracting, especially for people who have to concentrate or to do creative or considerative work. If you have a number of people working for you and you have a large open space, you have several choices. One is to scatter the work-stations (office desks, machines, laboratory benches or drawing boards, etc.) around the large room. The advantages are that people can see each other and communicate quickly and effectively. The disadvantages are likely to be noise and distractions, especially if they need to concentrate on what they are doing. Of course, noise can be reduced by sound-absorbing wall coverings, carpets and so forth. The other extreme is to have a series of floor to ceiling partitions to divide the space up into a series of little workshops, offices or laboratories. The advantages are that people can concentrate on what they are doing with fewer interruptions. The disadvantages are that you will probably need more space because you will need corridors and space around work-stations, whereas in the open plan these are to some extent the same. Communication between people will be reduced, which could be an advantage or a disadvantage.

A half-way house is to scatter the work-stations in the open space, and to have a series of partitions about five feet high to give people a measure of privacy and freedom from distractions. Combined with sound-absorbing carpets and some large pot plants such workplaces can combine the best of both worlds. This system also retains flexibility so that as your business develops and your needs change you can simply move the screens, machinery and desks around. You may need floor-to-ceiling partitions around a particularly noisy machine, and you may need one reasonably soundproof office for private interviews, although if you don't need this very often, alternative arrangements can usually be made, e.g. the coffee lounge of your local hotel.

Decoration and colour So far we have said little about the decoration and colour scheme. Most people like to work in a reasonably bright, clean room. Many factories nowadays are painted with bright pastel shades. Unless your business is very 'arty' it is probably best to avoid lurid colours and designs. Pipes that convey services like air, steam, hot water and so forth can be painted with the colour code. This is attractive as well as an aid to safety. The colour scheme you choose is largely a matter of personal preference, but do make sure that doors and objects are easy to see.

Security

Another aspect of the premises is security. First of all, the security of the clothes and belongings of your staff. If your offices are in a public building, for example, the sneak thief can quickly nip in and make off with handbags, portable radios and any loose cash. If that is a real danger you should provide some lockable cupboard or drawer for each employee. They will also need somewhere to hang their outdoor clothes – where they are not likely to be damaged or dirtied. If your people need to change clothes – for example to change into boiler suits or uniforms – you will need to provide full clothes lockers.

You may have reason to take precautions concerning bomb threats and letter bombs. In such cases the police are ready to give you advice. You should always take a bomb threat seriously and take appropriate action. The appropriate step is generally to raise the alarm and to evacuate the building. The position of the suspected bomb, however, must be considered. If the bomb is believed to be in one of the main exit routes, e.g. on a staircase, steps must be taken to evacuate by alternative routes.

If any of your equipment or materials are readily portable and saleable, you will need to train your staff to take reasonable precautions and, where appropriate, provide secure cupboards and drawers. You should, of course, be especially careful if you ask your staff to carry much currency or other readily disposable valuables to the bank or other premises.

So much for the premises themselves. If you decide that the time has come to acquire different premises, there are other matters to consider in addition to those listed above. You will want to consider, in particular, the environment of the premises and the ease with which your staff and any new people you may employ, can travel to work. We are here concerned with the premises from the viewpoint of the staff. There may be sound commercial reasons which may be of over-riding importance, e.g. you may want your shop near a busy pedestrian area, or your factory near a railway goods yard. But from your employee's point of view, the general ambience of the neighbourhood, the ease of travelling and the proximity of shops are probably paramount factors. Many people like to pop out at lunch-time and buy some groceries and other supplies. Do not underestimate the importance of this matter if you want to recruit and retain good staff. A green field, cows and birds are all very well, but if that means that all the shopping has to be done on Saturday, your workplace may not be as popular as you would wish.

Note The main laws relating to premises and equipment are listed below. There are also numerous regulations. These are liable to be changed from time to time and you will need to get up-to-date information.

Factories Act, 1961.

Offices, Shops and Railway Premises Act, 1963.

Employers' Liability (Compulsory Insurance) Act, 1969.

Employers' Liability (Defective Equipment) Act, 1969.

Fire Precautions Act, 1971.

Health and Safety at Work etc. Act, 1974.

Action Guidelines

1 Have you made sure that your premises comply with the relevant regulations? (See Note on page 47.)

2 Have you had a walk round lately to check on sources of danger?

3 When did you last have a fire drill?

4 Have you taken out proper insurance policies?

5 Have you considered what it is like to work in the various places where you expect your people to work?

6 If you contemplate a move, have you considered possible new locations from the viewpoint of your people?

5
Looking Ahead with People

- People need time to adjust to change.
- There are many steps you can take to prepare people for change and to help them to cope with it.
- You will need to inform them and to consult them for their views. But you must choose the timing and subject matter for discussion carefully.
- The more open you can be with people the better.
- Sometimes you will have to negotiate. Prepare thoroughly for this, and do all you can to see that both sides feel satisfied at the outcome.

Problems of change

Most people don't like too much change to happen quickly. They feel safer if any changes in the place where they work, the people they work with or the work itself are slow and foreseen well in advance. People can, of course, adapt to dramatic changes in these areas, but each change adds a little to the stress people feel. It is not surprising, then, to find that when a manager suddenly announces that the firm will make new products, introduce new machines, move to another site or have a new supervisor, people feel apprehensive.

Fear of change This feeling of apprehension – or even fear – is quite natural. The manager must reckon with this and be careful to introduce such changes in ways that are, as far as possible, acceptable to the people who work for the outfit. Even if it is necessary to make changes that are bound to be unpopular, it is possible to minimize people's apprehension and its consequences. When people are fearful about their jobs (or indeed about most things) there are two typical kinds of response. Crudely, these can be summarized by 'fight – or flight'. Of course, generally speaking, people at work don't raise their fists to hit the manager, but they can become hostile, firstly to the proposed changes and then to the people who are initiating or implementing them. The manager who meets this hostility merely with toughness is heading for a confrontation. Indeed his or her own toughness is probably an apprehensive reaction in itself!

The manager must not, however, run away from the problem or ignore it. The other typical response to fear is flight. Once again people do not generally pack up and run away – although sometimes they do just that, either in some form of industrial action or by leaving the firm. But they can withdraw their goodwill, their enthusiasm and their keenness to see the work done well. In most firms really good, cost-effective work depends as much on the goodwill of the workers as it does on the planning and systems of the management. That's why it is a serious threat for workers to say they will work to rule. This implies, often justifiably, that you can get more done by bending the rules here and there than by sticking to the systems laid down by management. (Of course, no one can tolerate the bending of sensible safety and health rules.)

If you as a manager try to introduce some profound change without proper consideration for the likely reaction of your employees – or your partners or co-directors – don't be surprised if you get a hostile or an apathetic reaction. You may be able to work through it, and to allay their fears, but the effectiveness of your enterprise will be diminished while it is being sorted out. If you are in such a position, the best way forward is to let people have their say to you, preferably in small groups, one or two at a time. If you get everybody together they may well encourage each other to magnify the problem out of all proportion and to convince themselves that you are an insensitive, overbearing tyrant! Then you must listen to what people have to say and take into account the fears and anxieties they talk about – even if these are expressed in hostile words and ways. Some of these anxieties will be groundless. Patiently explain why this is so. Some of the fears may be based solidly on something that will happen to change their working lives in ways they do not like or understand. It's no good brushing these fears aside or trying to explain them away. Face up to them. See what you can do to make the change more acceptable or more understandable to them. For example, they may be afraid of some new equipment to be introduced, thinking that it will reduce them to mindless machine minders doing dull, repetitive work. If that is untrue, take them to see the machine working in someone else's factory. If it *is* true, you must help them come to terms with it, or think of ways of reducing the boredom and repetition.

Prepare for change

But what we have been talking about in the last few paragraphs is fire-fighting. It is about taking action after the fear has taken over and the hostility and/or apathy and withdrawal has set in. You must learn how to cope when 'fire' breaks out, because even with the best will in the world problems will come along, sometimes not of your making and sometimes by your oversight. Some of these will cause your people to be apprehensive. So learn to recognize the signs and to control your own reaction so that you may work constructively for a solution, and not blunder into a confrontation that will sap your energy and deplete the reserves of your enterprise. It is far better to foresee the problem and to carry people with you. That is what leadership is all about.

Informing   So then what does it come down to if you want to lead people, and to manage them when change and challenge is in the air? In essence it means treating people like people. It means giving them as much notice as you can about future plans and acitivities – including frank statements about uncertainties, e.g. about contracts you may or may not get, and your honest appraisals of the way things are going. Don't play the martyr and nurse all your worries, putting on a bold face 'for the troops'. They will soon see through this kind of sham. The real worry is that they will wrongly interpret your secretiveness, and come to believe that what you are hiding is not genuine business problems, but a personal plot which is to their disadvantage. If you generally adopt an open, honest policy, they will almost invariably accept the fact that there are some bits of information which must be kept confidential – like the price you quoted on your current tender to a major customer. On the whole the more open you are with people, the more ready they are to trust you with that special business secret for the good of the firm.

Consulting   But there is more. As well as just telling your people what is likely to happen, you can seek their views about it. The extent to which you can consult will vary enormously according to the issues involved. But do try to err on their side. Let them give their views as much as you possibly can. You may be amazed at the very helpful advice and comments you will get if you do this. If you have not completely fouled up your relationships, people will respond positively to the opportunity to contribute ideas and suggestions. Try to encourage ideas that go beyond the immediate tasks and responsibilities of the people concerned. They may well have something useful to say about another area of the business or about some wider issues. I have often been surprised at what good ideas have come from young people, or from people in mundane jobs who have worked for me.

People can be at their most helpful, however, when you ask them to consider how the changes are likely to affect their work, and how they relate to other people in the firm. Don't forget that any change looks different from different places. What may seem helpful to you, may be full of snags for some of your people. Work with them on the problem. Listen to them and take as much of their advice as you can. Many of their suggestions will cost little more than the way you would have chosen to do it anyway, and their goodwill in the future will probably more than compensate for the marginally extra expense. You may well find that some of their suggestions will bring about a genuine improvement for the firm and the worker concerned and even save money. If someone makes a suggestion which you can't go along with, say so. Don't fudge it. Do your utmost to explain why. Ultimately you must say that you have listened carefully, but that although they have put forward a good argument up to a point, you simply can't agree. Don't belittle the idea if it was genuinely offered.

Whatever you do, be sincere. If you consult your people – asking for their views – be sure to take notice. Do your utmost to accept some of the advice – and be seen to do so. There's nothing to be ashamed about, and it does not make you any less a manager or a leader. But do not, for goodness sake, consult if you don't intend to take any notice.

Negotiating Just as consultation is more time-consuming (and energy-consuming!) than informing, there is a further step, i.e. negotiating. This is where you want your people to agree to something, but realize that you will have to pay a price for it. Do you want to move the factory 20 miles away, but take your key people with you? You may want the people who don't move to leave the firm peaceably, and in some cases to keep working until you are almost ready to shift the machinery. You will want the work to continue as smoothly as possible up to and after the move. What will the people want in return? Do not try to work it all out in detail on your own. Inform, consult, negotiate. The way you negotiate will be a function of the size of your outfit and the extent to which your people belong to trade unions. Whether you negotiate with them individually or through representatives, you will need to have a lot of patience and you will need to learn how to listen carefully to recognize the areas of common ground, the sticking points and the room for manouvre. We shall return to the skill of listening later (Unit 9), and negotiating skills are considered below in this Unit.

- Don't forget that the essence of successful negotiations is that everyone comes out feeling that they have won. It's what some Americans call the win-win outcome.
- It is not good business in the long run for you to win, if your staff feel that they have lost.
- Honourable people will stick to the agreement, but don't expect any enthusiasm, and don't be surprised when they refuse to stretch a point for you, like staying on a few minutes or working overtime when there's a rush on.

This does not mean that everyone comes out of a negotiating position having got all they want. It means they emerge feeling that they have got a good deal taking into account all the circumstances. Remember that bit about circumstances, and do notice that the word 'feelings' comes into this a lot. People can leave the negotiating table with a good deal – but feel its a poor one! You need to take these factors into account as you prepare to enter negotiations.

So far we have not mentioned employee representatives. If your employees are members of a trade union that has secured bargaining rights with you as an employer, you will also wish to use this established machinery to inform your people of new developments and changes. Do notice the word 'also'. It is a mistake to rely on the trade unions as the vehicle for informing the workforce about changes, especially in very small firms. Tell your senior people your ideas first, then tell your people yourself. If you have an agreement with a trade union this probably includes a section about informing them of proposed changes. Indeed, an employer has a duty to disclose to the representative of a trade union recognized by him, information necessary for the purpose of collective bargaining. This corresponds to good industrial relations practice.

Joint decision-making There is yet another level at which you can involve people in management decisions. You can bring them in and make the decision together – jointly. This is much more difficult than informing, consulting or negotiating. The key reason why it is hard is because good joint decisions should be based on a common or a shared interest. Negotiating is when two people or two groups of people need to 'trade-off' rewards. Let's look at it this way. If two hungry men in the forest want to catch and kill a deer then their discussion about how to go about it and the decisions they make are based on a common objective – to get some food. Once they have caught it and killed it they will need to share it out. If they are very hungry and greedy then each one might try to get more than the other. Any discussion now is on a different basis since one man can only get more at the expense of the other. This is not a good basis for joint decisions, but involves negotiation!

Many instances where people set up what they call joint decision-making machinery suffer from this flaw. The people who meet often find it difficult to look objectively at decisions for the good of 'the firm' (which can mean different things to different people), without considering how the change will affect them personally and their workmates, if they represent them. This means that if you really want to involve people positively in joint decisions, you must take steps to identify issues where there is a real common interest, and take the trouble to see that all those involved really understand what is going on. If, for example, you ask your machine operatives to talk about the improved cash flow you want to achieve, make sure they know something about firms and money matters. That may be obvious, but it is often overlooked.

The more you can identify areas of common interest and discuss them with your people, the more commitment you will gain from them. Few things motivate more than clear, shared goals.

Preparing for consultation

So then how do you prepare yourself for this task of informing your people, consulting them, negotiating with them or involving them in joint decisions?

- Don't spring it on people suddenly in a burst of irresponsible enthusiasm. Their reaction to that will be instant suspicion. 'What's the boss up to?' will be the question in their minds if not on their lips. Go at it gently. Talk it over with your senior people first, individually or in small groups of two or three. Tell them you are considering informing and/or consulting your people about some very specific issues.
- Don't just ask them how things are going! Choose the issues on which you would welcome comment, and would be prepared to take into account constructive ideas – and where you would be prepared to listen to destructive criticism and work through it. Then set up a couple of meetings where you meet people, say six or eight at a time.
- Don't have big meetings or long ones. Tell people what it's about and why you've called the meeting. Explain the issue or the problem, say you'll welcome comments but you can't promise to act on every one of them. Let people have their say, but don't let the meeting go on too long. Often it's better to have the meeting without chairs and keep to about 15 to 25 minutes. Chairs encourage people to be expansive rather

than incisive, and for this purpose long meetings are often no better than short ones – generally worse. If you sense genuine apprehension, hold another meeting a week or so later rather than having a long meeting. The aim must be to keep these sessions brief, alive and vital, not long and boring. Then you must go away and consider what's been said.

- Don't make promises on the spur of the moment or enter into commitments you have not had time to think about. Nothing undermines confidence more than managers who can't deliver. What you *can* commit yourself to do is to consider carefully all that has been said and to investigate any serious problem that was raised.

But there is a catch. Now you have started you *must* follow through, consider the ideas and investigate the complaint or whatever, and *report back* to the group within a reasonable time. Having asked for their views you now owe them an explanation of what difference, if any, that consultation made. If you don't follow through you will find it ten times harder next time – when you may really need their support.

Suppose you find it necessary to negotiate. There are text books and courses on this, but here we shall look at the subject in simple terms. Informing and consulting are skills which you might develop on your own or with a little help. It's much harder to develop negotiating skills quickly on your own and if this is a serious issue for you, perhaps you should take a few days out to do a course. Anyhow, let's look at the basics now.

Preparing for negotiating

The current position Before you go to a meeting where you expect to negotiate, get out a sheet of paper. Start by making a few brief notes on the relevant *current* position. If you're not sure about any important facts, check up on them before the meeting (see Figure 9). Your position is considerably weaker if you get into a meeting and get caught out by not being sure about the relevant facts.

Figure 9 *Preparing for negotiation*

My perspective

1 *The basic facts now.*
2 *My objectives* (what I want to get out of the negotiations).
3 Why do I want these objectives?
4 What will happen if I do not achieve my objectives?
5 What am I prepared to pay for my objectives?

The other people's perspective

6 How are the facts likely to appear to them?
7 What are likely to be their reactions to each of your objectives?
8 What are they likely to want out of the negotiations?

Comparisons

They want	I am prepared to give
1	1
2	2
3	3

I want	They are prepared to give
1	1
2	2
3	3

Objectives Then write down just what you aim to get out of the negotiation. You might find it useful to jot down – in note form – just why you want to do it. You will find this useful in two ways. It should help you to clarify your objectives more precisely and to know what room for manouvre you have if alternative ideas come along in discussion. Secondly, you may be asked why you want to change. You will need to be ready with a clearly thought out reply. You can't expect to succeed if you seem to be in a muddle about the essential point of the whole exercise. You may find it useful to ask yourself *why* again – to your first answer to the question. It is sometimes enlightening to push your own thinking more deeply. You want to move ten miles away, for example. *Why?* Because storage space is cheaper, perhaps. So you really want to save money on storage space? Someone might ask you if you could work with lower

57

stocks and save yourself (and your staff) the trouble, expense and upheaval of moving. When you get down to the basic problem you may find alternative solutions – or your people might suggest them.

Failure to achieve objectives Next question – what will happen if I fail to achieve my objectives? For example, if you fail to persuade your staff to co-operate with you in a relocation situation you could find your business being poorly run and people claiming excessive compensation or whatever. That's one kind of answer. Alternatively, you might conclude that if you don't get their co-operation on some issue or another the firm will lose money and have to close down. Be very careful indeed how you use such information, e.g. as a threat. If it is a genuine assessment of the situation you may need to spell it out. On the whole it is better to gain co-operation by accentuating the positive side rather than by emphasizing threats or impending doom. You can cry wolf too often.

Get your objectives broken down:
- Are some more vital than others?
- What are you prepared to pay to achieve your objectives? (After all, you want something which your people may not see as in their best interests).
- If they meet your objectives, what will they get in return?
- What are you prepared to offer?

Other people's perspective Now it's time to put yourself in the other person's place:

- What will the negotiation look like from the other end?
- Are the other people likely to see things differently – in terms of the current situation, for example?
- Are there some facts known to you and not to them?
- Are there some facts they will have, but you do not?

For example, they might have consulted people in other firms or through their unions to find out what normally happens in such cases. If you fail to consider such possibilities you may find yourself at an embarrassing disadvantage in the negotiating situation.

The next thing to do is to make a note of their likely reactions to each of your objectives. Some they may find acceptable, some they may be non-committal about and some they may be hostile to. If you think about all this you are less likely to be wrong-footed. If you are dealing with a very experienced negotiator, be careful. His arrangements may not follow your kind of logic, but he has a logic of his own, i.e. what ploys can he use to extract the very best deal for his members. Don't expect arguments based on the good of the firm to carry a great deal of weight here.

What are they likely to want out of the negotiations? Don't forget that in exchange for giving you what you want they may ask for something quite disconnected with the matter in hand, especially if they are not really concerned much about the proposed change, but know that it matters to you. Itemize the demands you can anticipate. then ask yourself which demands they are likely to feel strongly about, and the ones for which they will probably not press hard.

The last bit of preparation is to set out on paper your objectives against their reactions and their demands against what you are prepared to offer. Look for all the areas where agreement is likely and for areas where you can see a compromise which will probably be acceptable to both sides. Then study the items on which sharp disagreement is likely. Think through how far you are really prepared to go and how far you consider the other folk will bend. Ultimate success depends on finding an acceptable deal on these issues.

The meeting Now you're ready for the meeting. Meet around a table in a pleasant room. Harsh surroundings make people less amenable to reason. Don't encourage people to drink alcoholic beverages. It befuddles the mind and increases hostility in some people. If more than two people are involved, you may find it helpful, at intervals, to encourage each 'side' to go off for a private word amongst themselves. See that another pleasant room nearby is free for such purposes. Remember that the aim is to come to an honourable, amicable agreement where each side feels they have won. Scoring 'points' in discussion may give you a temporary sense of satisfaction, but it scarcely takes the negotiation forward if it's done in a belligerent manner. Remember that people take time to change their minds over important issues. Allow time for people to reflect over alternatives. Don't try to rush agreements. It's a good idea to spread negotiations over a series of meetings at intervals. When you have reached agreement, make sure this is clearly spelt out in the meeting and written down. Then each side must study the text carefully to make sure it expresses properly what was agreed. Now you must honour your side of the bargain and expect others to do the same.

Action Guidelines

1 As each idea for change comes along, consider who you will inform. consult or negotiate with about it. Think about the stages at which different people need to be brought into the picture.

2 Before you enter into negotiation consider how you will prepare for it.

3 Think about your relationships with trade union or staff representatives, if they exist in your firm. How will you communicate with them on a regular basis?

6
How to Set Targets

- **Where it is appropriate, setting targets at a realistic level can help to stimulate and motivate people.**
- **Be sure your targets are really in line with your business requirements.**
- **Be careful not to take too mechanistic or narrow a view in setting targets.**
- **Ensure the targets different people have add up to an effective whole.**
- **Targets are no use if there is no proper follow-up and review at appropriate intervals.**

Target levels

People generally work best when they have clear targets which they can achieve. This is true whether the goals are in terms of making things or learning things. If a person believes that the target cannot be achieved, then all the heart goes out of the effort. Notice that the word 'believes' comes into this. It is not enough that the achievement is technically feasible, the people concerned must believe in it.

On the other hand, targets that can be attained without real effort often lead to slackness and a lack of motivation to succeed. Most of us need to be reaching out a little, struggling a little, pushing forward a little. This element of feeling stretched is healthy and keeps us on our toes. This must not, however, be confused with being overloaded, or with appearing very 'busy' without achieving very much. We must always be on our guard against activity as a substitute for achievement, and we must ensure that the people who work for us are not subjected to over-heavy workloads.

Emergencies Most people can be pushed hard in the short run to cope with a genuine emergency. If they have been treated decently in the normal run of business, they will most likely be happy to work for longer hours when the crunch comes. But this is no excuse whatever for pushing people hard all the time. On the contrary, under these circumstances they have nothing extra to give in an emergency, and may be too work-weary to pull out the stops.

Clear targets A word on the need for clear targets. This does not mean that the targets must always be very precise. There are a number of jobs and tasks where precise goals are easy to define – like the number of cabinets produced each day, the number of telephone sales achieved each week or the speed with which mail orders are turned around. You may well find that there are some jobs and tasks like that in your own firm. It may be a good idea to identify these.

Before you rush out and assign numerical values to targets in each case, just remember two things.

- Will the target figure you assign be acceptable to the job-holder?
- Are there other features of the job or task which you can't count up in numbers, but which are just as important to the success of your firm?

There is the important question of **quality**, for example, and how you write this into your goals. It's no good having achieved a target of 10 cabinets a day if half of them are badly made or finished. Of course, a simple way out of this is to say that the number 10 refers to cabinets which conform to a certain level of quality which then has to be defined. For items like cabinets this is probably not too difficult, although there may well be marginal cases. The point is that there is often a trade-off between quantity and quality and your targets must take this into account.

What about the telephone sales example? In the short run your sales people might put psychological pressure on the purchasers and generate a number of orders. The likelihood is that such tactics will produce some orders for a short time. What your business needs are large orders repeated over and over again. How do you set targets that reflect both the size and the likelihood of repeat orders? Once more, it can be done, but once again we can see that the simple-minded, quick answer may not be in the firm's best interest.

Similar considerations apply to the mail order firm. Speed of turn-around is fine, but the goods despatched must be correct, i.e. as ordered, well packed, properly addressed and stamped. Thus even in the simplest jobs the description of the target is not just a number.

In reality, especially in the smaller firm, many jobs are by no means that simple to quantify, and your targets will need to be broader and different for each member of your team. Many jobs will consist of a range of tasks, some of which will be more quantifiable than others. Some tasks may well defy any form of quantification. If you have a receptionist or someone to answer the telephone, the way in which they deal with enquiries may be very important indeed to your firm. How can you quantify such activities? Indeed is it sensible to try? But you can talk to the person concerned and agree that the target is that every enquirer should go away feeling that their needs have been considered sympathetically and met as far as possible. Such people are more likely to call again. By the way, this simple chat is not as easy as it sounds.

Judging by the variety of receptions one meets on the telephone or at front entrances, it seems that many bosses are either unaware or simply not interested in the way enquiries are handled. It is very impressive when you are confronted by a telephonist or receptionist who makes you feel that your enquiry is welcome (and not an intrusion) and will be dealt with properly. (By the way, it is not difficult to train people to use the telephone properly and coaching helps as well.)

Setting goals and targets for managers and supervisors needs flexibility and practice. Targets imposed by the boss without discussion can work, but they are more likely to arouse resentment – if they are seen as unfair or unworkable – or to lead to slackness if they are too easy. This argues strongly for some level of involvement by the people concerned. Different levels of involvement in decisions are covered in Unit 5. They apply here. There is, however, an added dimension to be taken into account, i.e. the way in which people depend on each other to achieve results.

If we take the telephone selling operation as an example, the sales people need a good list of names and telephone numbers to start with. It's no good asking them to sell pet dogs to people who live in high-rise flats! If the basic list of contacts is faulty – out-of-date or inappropriate – the telephone sales people don't stand a chance. They may have some good suggestions of their own about what names should be included and it may well be useful to involve them in compiling and revising these lists. Furthermore, if the firm does not provide good back-up literature and advertising (where appropriate) and then actually fulfil the orders promptly, the repeat orders will not flow. It is like that in your firm, most likely. Individuals can't achieve their targets if the spares are not available or the photocopier is not working or whatever. You need to look at the ways people depend on each other before you set targets.

Practicalities

So much for the introductory remarks. Let's get down to procedure. How do you set about setting targets? Don't go in for an elaborate system that takes up more time and effort than it is worth. If your firm has only a few people, setting targets is very important, but it must be kept in proportion. Look at Figure 10.

The starting point is the business.

- Write down in a list, the critical features of the business as you see it (column A). Don't worry about whether some are internal and others external factors or anything like that. Put down what concerns you.

- Make sure you write down what you think makes the difference between success or failure. The list of items might include the need to secure a flow of orders, to control cash flow, to control pricing policy, to ensure quality, to secure deliveries of raw materials on time, to meet delivery dates of your own finished goods, to schedule work flows, to monitor progress, to be prepared for crises, e.g. loss of power supply.

- Discuss the list with your top team and improve the list together.
- Ensure your list is complete, but don't fill it up with trivia.

The next thing to do is to satisfy yourself that someone considers himself or herself responsible to see that all is well in each of these areas. Jot down their initials in the right-hand column B. If two or more people have joint responsibility for some area, ensure that they agree on how this should be handled, and that you are happy with this arrangement. There are always dangers in this unless people's roles are clearly understood, even if they are highly flexible. The next thing to do is to think about where the important links are between different parts of your organization. How do sales tie up with production, production with purchasing and so on? In a very small firm there may be no problems. But even in firms employing only a dozen people communications break down. Be sensible about how you complete column C. If it's not a big issue in your firm, a few jotted notes and initials will suffice.

Reviewing targets

Now we move into the interesting part. For each key area choose a realistic time span for review. For the routine manufacture of small items you may want hourly targets. For the output of assembled bulky items a daily or weekly target might be more appropriate. For most of the jobs your managers and supervisors do, longer time spans of one, two, three or even six months may be more appropriate. You must distinguish between the time cycle for the operation and an appropriate period for review. In many smaller outfits a weekly review of performance in certain areas is most useful, but in such cases it is too easy to miss the wood for the trees. A longer time horizon, perhaps based on the trading year and with six-, three- and one-monthly targets may be needed to ensure success. Discuss the target time spans and decide on review dates. Make sure everyone knows who is expected to achieve what before the review date(s) and that they feel the goals are, with effort, achievable. Thus you can complete columns D to G.

Face to face discussion When the time comes for review, it is sound practice to talk to each of your subordinates alone first,

Figure 10 *Setting targets*

I Setting goals

A. Critical features of the business   B. Person(s) responsible   C. Linked features and people responsible

D. Performance in each area   E. Target time spans   F. Review date   G. Person(s) responsible

II Performance review

H. Performance expected   I. Performance achieved   J. Comments

III Review meeting

K. Areas for improvement   L. Action to be taken   M. Person(s) responsible   N. Review date especially if there has been difficulty in achieving the desired results. For most people it is not helpful for the boss to attack and criticize them in the presence of their peers. It is much better to iron out these problems in private, and in public to encourage your people to improve performance. Even in private, the important thing to remember is that if you want a good performance out of someone, don't destroy their self-esteem and self-confidence. If things have gone wrong, make sure you take into account problems that were beyond the control of the person concerned. If the individual made mistakes, or fell down on the job, encourage him or her to discuss these events with you. Make sure your discussion concentrates on the problem and on how such mistakes can be prevented in the future. (You may find it helpful to re-read Unit 1. It will not take long!)

A positive approach Of course, if you think someone has been deliberately obstructive, you may decide to have a showdown. Again, do it in private and only as a very last resort. If tempers are aroused both you and the other person may say things you don't really mean. They will be hard to live with later; even more so, if they are said at a meeting. Do think about what you hope to gain out of a review meeting. It's worth preparing the ground carefully, as described in Unit 5. Complete columns H, I and J. Some people seem to use meetings like this to let off steam. That is pure self-indulgence and unworthy of someone who wants to manage people well. If your aim is to improve people's performance and ability to achieve goals, be positive.

Having spoken to people individually, you should have discovered if there are any problems between people or different parts of the organization. This means that you can call a meeting of the top team and tackle some of the obstacles to success. But once again, be positive. Don't let people waste time looking for scapegoats. Focus on what went wrong and why, and what can be done about it by improving your system, your information flow or the allocation of responsibilities, or by helping individuals to make a better contribution through some appropriate training. Out of such discussions fresh goals should be forged, and written down (columns K, L and N).

The bigger and more complicated your firm is, the more detail you can put into these tables, but don't be tempted simply to fill up space. A few brief notes, initials and dates should prove a real help to you. Don't go beyond that unless you really believe there is a pay-off. Use the tables if you find them helpful.

We have not concentrated very much on numerical figures as targets because they can so easily be misused, diverting attention away from more important issues. Nevertheless they have their place and it is useful to keep track of numbers of items produced per hour or day or whatever. Such data can be used to monitor the operation of the production department, the effectiveness of advertising media (by coding the address you give for replies) and a host of readily quantified activities. It can also be used as hard data in the review discussions described above.

Action Guidelines

1 Where do you think target-setting can be useful to you?

2 Would it be useful to draw up a simple set of targets for the key people in your firm?

3 What advice will you give your senior staff as they think about target-setting for their subordinates?

4 How can you strike the right balance between the quality of products and the speed of production?

5 What steps can you take to see that quality is maintained?

6 In simple, repetitive operations, what can you do to set targets and also maintain interest in the job?

7 How can you make sure that targets are achieved?

7
How to Encourage People

- Have you thought about why people come to work at your particular firm?
- Do they stay with you or move on quickly?
- Do people leave, or do you have difficulty recruiting staff – why?
- Are people concerned about the way the firm is run?
- Do your people work with enthusiasm and are they really concerned to see that your products and services are of high quality?
- There are a number of steps you can take to encourage people to give of their best.

Why people come

Have you ever thought about why people come to work for you? The immediate reaction most people have to such a question is one word – money! Of course that is true. If you did not offer payment, you would probably have no workers. On the other hand if you have had any connection with voluntary work at all, i.e. in youth clubs or the social work of churches – you would soon discover that a lot of people will work for less tangible rewards. If you want to have a firm where people work enthusiastically, you had better consider some of these intangibles – whilst not forgetting the financial side of things. This book is primarily addressed to those who are trying to run a small enterprise commercially. This may not be for profit in the financial sense, although each of the people who have a stake in the enterprise will want a monetary reward, e.g. a salary or director's fee.

Let us accept then, that people come to work for you because they expect to receive financial rewards. But this does not explain why they come to work for you – as opposed to the shop down the road or the factory round the corner – unless, of course, you pay very high wages. The next question is, how long do people stay with you? Are you one of the employers who have people for years and years, people who you know and trust, and who you feel know and trust you? That's a good situation to be in – although in extreme cases an over-stable workforce can have its own drawbacks which you should take into account.

In later Units we shall be dealing with how to recruit people. So let us assume for the moment that you can persuade people to work for you and they seem to be happy to stay with you for a reasonable length of time. That, in itself, does not ensure that they will work enthusiastically and effectively. In talking about motivation at work many people confuse three separate – though interacting – issues. In this Unit we shall try to see the differences between them because if you can get a real sense of this you will be a far better manager and leader.

The three issues are:

- What persuades people to come and work for you?
- What discourages them from doing a good job?
- What encourages them to work enthusiastically?

Before you read on have a crack at completing the people checklist in Figure 11. If you were once employed yourself, you might get some clues from your own experience.

Some critical factors How did you get on with these four questions? You will get much more out of what follows if you had a go at them:

- Did you put money down first?
- Did you say anything about how easy it was for people to get work?
- Do your people have far to come?

Figure 11 *People checklist*

Why do people come
to work for my firm?
(List at least *seven*
reasons.)

Why do people leave
my firm? (List at least
five reasons.)

What discourages my
people from doing a
good job?

How can I encourage
my people to work
enthusiastically?

- What is public transport like, and car parking facilities?
- If your people have to struggle through the rush hour in each direction, have you considered flexitime or staggered working hours?
- Do people like it because you are near some good shops so that they can nip out for groceries at lunch-time?
- Is your firm located in a pleasant, quiet or beautiful position?
- Are the premises inviting – light and airy with adequate heating and ventilation, freshly painted with windows that open and toilets that flush?
- Is it a healthy place to work or do people think it is dangerous or regard it as a place where people seem to be away ill a lot?

In themselves, none of these items are likely to be decisive, but in people's minds they are often totted up as on a score-card, and with too many minus points your firm becomes a poor prospect. Then you might have taken a different line and talked about the friendliness of the people who work in your firm, the fact that they always have plenty to do without being worked to death or driven like slaves. You might have elaborated on your excellent bonus scheme, pension scheme, good holidays, luncheon vouchers, generous time off for dental appointments, or to look after sick children and so forth. I don't suppose you offer a cheap house-purchase scheme or interest-free loans for season tickets. Most people prefer to work in a friendly atmosphere, provided there is some real work to be done and that the whole time is not spent gossiping. Many people prize a good pension scheme. One factor you must consider is that what may appeal strongly to some people will not cut much ice with others. Not many teenagers are switched on by the prospects of a wonderful pension scheme! Once again these items will vary in importance and rarely will one of them be decisive, but they all add up when people decide where to work, and whether to stay there.

There is a further critical issue – the style of management:

- Do your employees see you as an autocrat who gives orders and expects instant, blind obedience, not caring for what they think and feel? (Of course not, you reply. Are you sure?)

- Do you seek people's views, ask them how they would tackle some jobs, try to sense their feelings and then make up your own mind, taking these things into account, and then expect people to follow your orders? What you might call a considerate autocrat.
- Do you feel that you have the best interests of your staff at heart and that your actions and intentions reflect this? You know what's good for your people and you give it to them, and expect in response that they will work well for you. What we might term a benevolent autocrat.

On the other hand you might be a person who likes to make decisions jointly with people, or to let people make decisions for themselves within reason. You might be termed to some extent a delegator, or a democratic decision maker. You notice that caveat – 'within reason'. Naturally there will be areas and issues upon which you alone will make the decisions, so what we are talking about is a question of degree and not kind. An effective manager should be able to vary the extent to which he delegates and shares decisions according to the circumstances. Managers who can never decide anything for themselves are more ineffective than those who decide everything, but be sure of this, a person who cannot delegate or share decisions will rarely get the best work from his people.

This may have seemed a digression. It is not. People are influenced in their choice of firm, and whether they stay there, on the basis of what they believe to be the management style. They may not use these words, but they will recount stories of the way people have been treated and from this – and from experience – they build up a picture of what it is like to work for J. Ash. How often have you heard it said over a pint at the local – 'They would not listen when Jack told them they were doing it all wrong' and so forth.

You will find some people who are content to work for an autocrat, benevolent or not, although mostly people like to work for a boss who listens, takes notice and delegates to a reasonable extent. The worst problems arise with managers who are inconsistent and less than honest.

Where is all this leading? One way forward is to expand the list into a checklist of points for consideration. You could profitably talk it over with your deputy over lunch, or with some of your key people. They may have useful points to add. But before you do that, read on to the end of this Unit as you will get more ideas on the way.

What discourages people

Let us move on to the second question. If people don't leave your firm very often you won't have much to say and be hard put to it to find five reasons. OK. Skip the next paragraphs. If you are concerned about why people leave, you may have some clues from the preceding paragraphs. Some of the more obvious reasons are advancement (more money, better promotion prospects, to widen experience and so forth), pregnancy (although many women now come back to work soon after their baby is born) or the family moving out of the district. There's not much you can do about these in most cases. Anyway, some movement is healthy for most firms.

- Were there some unsatisfactory reasons – from your point of view?
- Were the people who left bored, or, conversely, overworked?
- Did they feel underpaid and exploited?
- Did they feel they were treated unreasonably – for example refused compassionate leave, stopped some money unfairly, passed over for promotion or simply ignored?
- Did they have a row with somebody?

Of course, you may not know, but if you have a high labour turnover these are some of the things you should look into. Most likely the reasons will indicate something which will adversely affect the people who stay with you. There is a limit to which positive incentives can overcome people's feelings about unfair treatment or poor working conditions. If you are faced with a lot of absenteeism, this could be a warning sign. Neglect this and you will probably soon be facing labour turnover problems.

Turning to question three, we have covered a lot of the ground in dealing with the first two. What's left? One thing we have not spoken about in this chapter is the work itself. Hitherto we have assumed that the people who come to work for you have at least some interest in your line of business and the technology it employs. This means that a car mechanic, for example, would be happy to work in a workshop where an element of dirt, grease and noise was inevitable. A receptionist for a veterinary surgeon would be content to deal with customers who brought in lame dogs, sick cats and canaries who are off their food! Let's assume, for the moment, that you have recruited roughly the right people for the job (and we live in an imperfect world so they may not be absolutely right):

- How does the working day flow? Is it all fits and starts with long periods where people can knit or read the newspapers followed by sudden periods when everyone rushes around madly trying to cope? Not many people would put up with that for long – although some would.
- Are there sudden changes in procedures without due warning?
- Are there frequent, unexplained changes in policy?
- Are there processions of customers irritated by failures elsewhere in the organization?

Be sure there is a limit to the tolerance most people have to such occurrences. Most people like an element of stability in their jobs, combined with some variety, but not violent upheavals. People are discouraged by frequent changes in pace, procedure or policies. Although they may not leave the firm, the quality of their work and commitment to the enterprise will suffer.

What encourages people

We are now on to question four. Do you begin to get the point? Clean premises, fair management, good financial rewards and pension schemes and the like all help to create the conditions under which people work with a will. But they are not enough to make people really enthusiastic. How do we add that last ingredient of positive motivation? What did you put?

Let me say at once that I do not think there is a single answer. For most of us there are a mixture of reasons, and although one reason may be the most important for one job at one time, things could be different at another place and time. If you get to know your people well enough, you will come to discover how to motivate them in this positive way.

Doing the job well People enjoy doing something well, whether it is making a clay jug, making a good cup of tea, typing a clean letter, turning a good crankshaft or making a smooth landing in a Concorde. If you can build this sense of achievement into people's jobs it will make a difference. The trouble is that so often the tasks people do are just small pieces of large jigsaw puzzles, and they never see the whole picture. This is where **you, as the leader of a small firm, can really score over the managers of big firms.** In many cases your people can do complete jobs – from the receipt of the order to the despatch of goods, or from the metal sheet into the finished ash tray. Even where this is not possible because of the need for specialization, it should be easy to help people see the whole picture, and where their contribution fits in. You would often be surprised at the difference this makes.

Praise Then again most of us like to be praised, to have our efforts recognized. But we will soon see through someone who hands out praise like confetti without considering the worth of the work in question. The manager who is ready to acknowledge good work is reinforcing that sense of achievement referred to above. There is therefore a need to make opportunities to see how people are doing, but not like an inspector looking for faults, more like a parent looking for some encouraging signs of talent in his or her offspring. A manager who gives sensible praise is more likely to be heard when he has sensible criticism to offer – and we return to that in Unit 8. Suffice to say here and now that it is possible to correct people and to maintain their enthusiasm.

A measure of control People like to feel that things are under control and that they have a good measure of that control as far as it affects their work. The machine operative likes to feel that the manager has made proper arrangements to keep the machine working properly, the raw materials coming and that the work that passes from his or her hands will be dealt with sensibly and ultimately sold. But he or she also likes to feel some measure of control over the machine, the pace of work and the quality of output. This is not always possible. Automatic control systems may be more efficient, but we need to think afresh, perhaps, about the content of the job and the satisfactions to be derived from it. The same is true in office work. Even in routine jobs, the ability of the individual to exercise some measure of control and to feel some sense of responsibility will enhance motivation. Amongst your top team this is a most crucial issue. Here is where the art of delegation counts the most. Your top team will work best if you can give people a real measure of control over certain aspects of the business. Naturally you will want to build in certain safeguards and reporting systems so that you can keep all aspects of the firm in balance.

Most of us like to feel that we get on well with the people around us. Not everyone wants the constant company of people, indeed some people prefer to work alone much of the time. However, even people who work alone generally like to feel that when they are with people they fit in. This sense of being socially acceptable can often influence the quality of work. If it is accepted in the firm that people who do high quality work are the good guys and that people who slouch around doing as little as possible are letting the side down, this will have a very real influence. This emphasizes the need to cultivate team spirit as described in Unit 3.

You may find it helpful to encourage an occasional social event – a Christmas party or annual social. This is very much a matter of judgement. If it is properly organized it can help to cement relationships, but if it is done badly, relationships can be soured. It depends on your own personality and the other people who work in your firm.

Informing Finally, people like to know what's going on around the place. We mentioned above the problem of managers who change policy or procedures so often people don't know from one day to the next what is expected of them or what circumstances will confront them. This is demotivating. Conversely, if the manager discusses changes in work patterns and so forth ahead of time, it is often (though not invariably) possible to get people to work enthusiastically through periods of change. You can also use information as a positive encouragement. If one of your top team, for example, is performing well, you can tell him or her and follow this up with information, in confidence, about an idea you have for the future. Seek the manager's opinions and expertise. Not only will you be wiser, he or she will feel the effort has been rewarded, and will want to strive to maintain your confidence.

Action Guidelines

1 To some extent this Unit is covered by Figure 11. However it might be useful to consider the following questions.

2 How important do you consider items like salary, working environment and conditions of service in your firm? Are they adequate?

3 What really motivates people to do a good job? Is there a good team spirit? Is the work interesting? Could this interest be increased in some way?

4 Could you help your staff to be more effective by the way you deal with them? What advice or help will you give to your more senior people so that they can enthuse the staff who work for them?

8
How to Correct People

- In dealing with someone who has done something wrong, the aim must be to get them to behave correctly in future, not to relieve your feelings or frustration and anger, or to mete out some rough justice.
- When a mistake occurs, be careful not to rush to conclusions. Consider what went wrong and why.
- There is a need to understand why people sometimes become more prone to make mistakes.
- It may well prove valuable to probe some mistakes more deeply.
- As a last resort, if you are on firm ground, you may need to take disciplinary action.

Positive correction

It is never a good idea to treat adults as if they are children. That is particularly true when it comes to trying to correct someone at the workplace.

When you discover that someone is doing something wrong, there is one issue you must try to keep uppermost in your mind. How can you get that person to behave correctly in the future – whether you are watching or not? This raises a number of important matters to be considered related to how to get people to work effectively after they have been 'corrected'. There's a great deal more to correcting people than simply 'giving them a piece of your mind'.

When you have an idea of how to tackle the problem, it is worth considering how the other person is likely to react if you were to actually put into effect the action you contemplate. Put yourself in the other person's shoes:

- Would you do the right thing from then onwards after such correction?
- Would you do it enthusiastically – or grudgingly?
- Would you appreciate – or resent – the way it was handled?

Now there are many occasions when you have to correct people on the spur of the moment, and when there is no time to sit back and think about the most effective way to tackle the job. That is all the more reason why you should think about the issues when there is not a crisis around. Furthermore, when you have got the time, and this is often true when dealing with poor management decisions for example, you should certainly do the job as well as you can. The way you correct people can have a big impact on morale, motivation and the effectiveness of your enterprise.

The aim of this Unit is not so much to help you deal with one-off problems – although that is covered – but to give you some pointers to help you improve your ability to correct people and to maintain their enthusiasm and commitment.

Let's consider an experience you have had and see if you can learn something from it. Think about why a person makes a wrong decision or takes a wrong action. If you don't think about it, the chances are that you will take action that is quite useless – or even counter-productive.

As an exercise think of a recent incident where someone who works for you – let's call the person JD – did something you considered wrong-headed or cack-handed. Try to choose an incident that you found really disturbing, rather than something you found trivial. Jot down some of the key features of the incident – including, if you can remember – the day of the week, the approximate time and anything special about the circumstances, for example on a Thursday night before a bank-holiday weekend.

Reasons for mistakes

The next thing to do is to ask yourself why JD made this mistake in this instance. Is it a one-off mistake or part of a pattern of mistakes? We will came back to this issue later. Write down the probable reason for the error. But just think about what you have put down and see if there may not be another possible reason – one that you did not think of at first, but which after all could explain the facts.

Ability and skills   Did JD make the mistake through some lack of ability? Did JD have the knowledge and skills to actually do what was expected on this occasion? It's not much good shouting at someone if they have never been taught properly how to use the machine or to make decisions of that kind. We touched on this issue in Unit 1. If the person can acquire the ability, and if similar situations are likely to recur, then the corrective action is training, coaching or some other learning experience. All you can say to the person concerned is that you see that a mistake has been made and you're sure that with a bit of coaching or training it can be avoided in future. There's no need to fudge the issue, but do bear in mind that you as a manager are substantially responsible for the incident if you put a member of your staff into a situation for which he or she was not prepared. Please note that I have avoided the use of the word 'blame'. We are not looking for a scapegoat or a culprit. We are trying to solve a problem and to make the business more effective. People who feel guilty – or who believe that other people think they are blameworthy – are not the easiest of people to motivate.

But you may be quite satisfied that, under normal circumstances, JD would be quite capable of taking the correct action. You then have to ask yourself what went wrong on this occasion? There are several possible answers, and appropriate remedial action will be different in each case. On that particular occasion JD's concentration may have been less than one hundred per cent. He or she may have had something else dominating his or her thoughts – or merely been physically unwell.

Stress   Both men and women have problems that can affect the quality of their work. It is well known that a number of changes in circumstances produce stress. If these changes come in ones and twos, people cope quite well. When three, four or five come close together in time, that stress can build up to the level where health is affected or concentration becomes difficult to maintain. The kinds of changes we are talking about are moving home, getting married (or divorced), changing jobs and death of a close relative.

People can cope with two of these close together without much aggravation, but three or four can sap their energies. In such cases the individual concerned needs support and encouragement, not a severe telling-off. Although it is wise to be broadly aware of the kinds of outside problems faced by the members of your staff, you should not try to be an amateur psychologist helping them to sort out these problems. They most likely have friends who can help them, and experts can be called upon where necessary. Your concern is with that person at work, and it is in this situation where you can help them to cope and succeed.

There are other external factors which can influence people's ability to concentrate on the job – money worries, sick relatives, the aftermath of a car accident and so on. There is probably very little you can do about these, but sometimes this can lead to people drinking too much hard liquor and arriving back at work after lunch the worse for drink. When this occurs as the result of some calamity, work colleagues often find ways to cover for the person concerned, and to make excuses. Up to a point such comradely behaviour is commendable. Unfortunately, however, if this goes on for too long the person concerned can develop a serious drink problem which is never an easy situation to handle. I know of no sure-fire ways of dealing with this. The individual concerned, and the family, friends and you, the boss, must all face up to the problem and try to work through it. The longer it goes on the worse it gets. Specialist agencies like Alcoholics Anonymous have experience and may need to be called in by the family or the individual. It is not your place to do this, and it would probably not help at all if you did.

Quite apart from the various external factors we have discussed, you may have put down as a possible reason for the mishap some factor within the firm. JD may be bored with the job, fed up with the environment or the people, or misunderstand what is expected. These are all areas where you can and should take a direct interest, and most probably take action. The extent to which people get bored and make mistakes varies enormously from person to person. Provided they can chat with their co-workers nearby, some people can happily beaver away daily at repetitive jobs which would irritate other people to distraction! The boredom of a group of people doing similar repetitive jobs can often be partially relieved by moving them around. For example, if a group of four people work at different places on an assembly line, they can move to different work-stations from time to time.

There are some jobs where boredom can lead to expensive or dangerous mistakes. (Most dangerous mistakes are also potentially expensive as well.) There is little point in blaming the people doing the jobs. The remedy may well lie in the way the work is laid out, the flow arranged and the tasks divided up. Whole books have been written on this subject, and here we can do no more than alert you to the problem and give you some clues. If you have this kind of problem at a serious level, perhaps you should seek expert help. The investment could be worthwhile.

Giving more responsibility You may find that you can enrich people's jobs, giving them more responsibility. Before you do this, however, there are two very important things to consider. Have they the ability to accept this responsibility, and who was doing it before? On the first point, you must see that the people concerned are adequately prepared by training and coaching to shoulder the new responsibilities. On the second issue, if you push responsibility down from someone who is overloaded with other interesting work (you or one of your senior managers), everybody probably gains. But if you push responsibility down and leave one of your managers or supervisors without enough interesting work to do, you may have helped solve one problem only at the expense of creating another. You notice the word 'interesting'. Making decisions and having responsibility is to many people rewarding and interesting. To take these away from a manager and to give them to his or her subordinates may leave the manager with plenty of work, but if it is now unbalanced in favour of administrative chores, motivation will suffer. The best solution in such cases is to enrich the manager's job itself, as well as that of the subordinates. Another thing to remember about delegation is that there are varying degrees of involvement which you can adopt, rather similar to the consultative process discussed in Unit 5.

Lack of information The reason you may have put down for the error is that the person concerned did not appreciate what the task was really about, or did not know some critical fact. Let us take a simple, trivial example. Suppose one Monday your clerk put on a hundred letters postage stamps which were insufficient in value because the price had been raised over the weekend. For some reason the clerk may not have heard about the increased cost of postage. It is no good blowing up – even if ten thousand letters were involved! The damage has been done. Your first priority is to prevent a recurrence on Tuesday. Do not, for goodness sake, set up a system to prevent this happening next year or whenever the next postal increase is likely to occur. Simply ask the clerk to gently keep a watch out for such things in future.

Analysing mistakes

We could go on thinking up reasons and talking about what action would be appropriate in each case. But the idea is not to build up an inventory of likely causes and plausible cures, but to illustrate the kind of thinking that could help you be a really effective manager and leader of your people. If you find it helpful, you may like to try the whole exercise again using a simple table like that shown in Figure 12. The way to use this table is to describe the incident –

Figure 12 *Correcting errors*

Incident	Possible reasons	Possible actions	Probable outcomes

telegram style – in the left-hand column. Then write down in the next column what you think may have caused the incident. Try to come up with more than one reason if you can.

The next step is to think through what action you might take. List one or two alternatives. Lastly, ask yourself how the people concerned are likely to react to each course of action you have described. Then recall your prime objective – to prevent recurrence. To this I would add a second aim which together with the first one is the real key to effective correction. You must help the person concerned to retain their self-confidence and enthusiasm. We will deal more fully with this later when we deal with the face-to-face interview.

At some point you have to talk to the person who has made the blunder. This can be an informal friendly word of advice and correction without undue strain on either side, especially if little harm has been done and no one has been injured. At the other extreme you may have to discipline somebody, or even sack them.

A formal interview   Obviously if the mistake has been repeated or the damage is serious, then a more formal interview must be arranged. Do prepare carefully for this. Do not make it more unpleasant than it has to be. Such extreme action is normally the result of one of two factors: gross incompetence, or deliberate malpractice. They need to be dealt with differently. In a small company such events will occur very rarely and so you cannot expect to have a lot of experience in dealing with them. If it comes down to disciplinary action or to termination of employment you would be wise to check out the legal position. Mistakes can be very costly in financial as well as human terms.

In cases of gross misconduct or of persistent misconduct you are justified in terminating a person's employment. In each case, however, you must be sure of your ground and have the evidence to back it up. In the case of persistent misconduct of a minor nature, you should give warnings by word of mouth first and later written warnings before you come to the ultimate step of dismissal.

In these earlier interviews, try to be positive and forward-looking. Seek for solutions. Try to establish areas of common ground for agreement as a basis for working together in the future. If you are unfortunate enough to have employed a rogue you cannot reform, you must ultimately accept the consequences. Often, however, people who make mistakes, even repeatedly, can be helped to see how to work positively and constructively if you can remove the obstacles to efficiency and provide the right incentives.

I have often spoken of this 'correction' interview as a one-to-one situation. This is generally the best. If you do lose your temper and say things you do not mean and afterwards might regret – or have to retract – better not to have an audience. In any case both you and our mythical 'JD' will have a tendency to 'play to the gallery' and justify yourselves if others are present. That's not a good way to start mending fences and building a fruitful future working relationship.

There are occasions when two or more of your people are involved in such an incident. At some point you will need to get them together. Again the people involved will tend to try and blame each other in front of the boss, especially if you are not careful to discourage this. It may be better for you to start by getting the facts from each person concerned alone. This will be the place for them to let off steam – in private. If you do this job well, then you can bring the folk concerned together and start off immediately looking to the future. Stress that your business is not to allocate blame but to prevent a recurrence – and of course to sweep up any mess lying around. You will be able to move quickly into this way of working if your team-building (Unit 3) has made some progress.

When you have to tell people off, individually or as a group, it is always better to concentrate on the deed, the action and the circumstances rather than on the question of individual or collective blame. The line to take is not 'what an incompetent idiot you are to do this', but rather 'how could an able person like you make a mistake like that?'.

Whatever way you try to correct people's behaviour, remember the two cardinal points:

- Look forward to how you can avoid trouble in future.
- Help people to retain self-respect.

Deliberate misbehaviour

We have tended to assume so far that the misbehaviour is not persistent and deliberate. If you are confronted with wilful indolence, obstruction or destructive behaviour, you must on no account ignore it. First of all see if there are some circumstances – poor management, unresolved genuine grievances or whatever which should be dealt with to remove any reason – or excuse – for such behaviour. Then take the individual aside and make it very clear, in private, that you are not prepared to accept this behaviour. If this does not prove effective you may need to initiate disciplinary procedures (see Unit 16 on the newcomer). The key thing to remember is the need to behave reasonably in all the circumstances.

Disciplinary action If you are forced to consider using your firm's disciplinary procedure you must be careful to establish facts and, where appropriate, to collect statements from witnesses. (You might find yourself before an industrial tribunal in the end.) If you consider that the misconduct warrants suspension, you should continue to pay the employee concerned, and this suspension should be kept as short as possible – just long enough to allow the case to be investigated. Before any decision is made or any penalty imposed, the employee must be interviewed, be afforded an opportunity to state his case and be advised of his rights under the disciplinary procedures in force.

If the offence is minor, give the individual a formal, oral warning and make a careful note about it. For a more serious offence, give the person a written warning, setting out what might happen if the offence is repeated. Keep a copy of the written warning and make a careful note of what happens.

If the person persists, then a further final written warning should be given stating that a further offence will lead to suspension, dismissal or some other penalty – as specified in your firm's disciplinary procedure. Finally, provided this is an express or implied condition of employment, you may take the last step of dismissal or a period of suspension without pay. You need to be on very firm ground in either case and you would be wise to check on the current state of the law. The employee is entitled to receive a written explanation of any penalty imposed. On rare occasions a misconduct may be so gross that it warrants dismissal the very first time it happens. Needless to say, if you find yourself in such a position you need to be very sure that you are fully justified in taking such action and that you can demonstrate this subsequently – with statements from witnesses wherever possible.

Action Guidelines

1 What are the key points to bear in mind if you are going to talk to someone about things that have gone wrong?

2 What action will you take if someone is deliberately indolent or destructive?

3 What records will you keep if you have to speak to people about misbehaviour?

4 What records will you keep if you have to issue written warnings or impose penalties?

5 Who, other than yourself, may deal with the kinds of issues raised above?

9
How to Talk and Listen

- It is important to be sure that people understand what you say and that you understand those with whom you work day by day.
- There are simple steps you can take both to improve your ability to get your message across and to be better at grasping what people are saying to you.
- If you have meetings, e.g. with two or three senior people, it is all too easy to waste time.
- There are different reasons for holding a meeting and it is important to be clear about what you are trying to achieve, and then to see that the way the meeting is run fits into this pattern.
- Inappropriate behaviour at a meeting can be counter-productive.
- There are ways in which you can become sensitive to what is happening in a meeting and get it on the right tracks.

Two-way process

Most of us think that we know how to talk. We have been doing it since we were little children. Nevertheless we are often surprised to find that people have misunderstood what we have said. In this Unit we are not concerned so much with elegant speech, but with the ability to get your message across to people – whether it is to your customer, your partner, your employees and so forth. We shall concern ourselves here with the spoken word – and all the non-verbal signals that can reinforce, diminish or confuse the spoken word.

But communication is a two-way process. If you want to find out whether your message has been understood you will need to listen and to observe. Once again you probably think you know how to listen – after all you have been doing it all your life, unless you are unfortunate enough to have defective hearing. But there is something more to listening to people than merely hearing the sounds they make and distinguishing the words they utter. At this deeper level a deaf person may be as good as a person with sound hearing when it comes to getting clearly the full import of what someone is trying to say. How often have you said to someone 'Are you willing to do such and such for me?', and received the reply 'Yes, I'll do it'. But somehow although the words are right, there's something about the tone of voice, the furrowed brow and the pursed lip which makes you think again. You begin to wonder whether the other person is really willing to do that little job, or whether they will, in the event, find any excuse to avoid it. If you are one of those people who just ignores all these non-verbal signals and ploughs on, or worse still if you don't even notice them, you really need to work on this problem. You will come a cropper one of these days.

When people misunderstand you, or when you fail to appreciate what others are trying to communicate to you in one way or another, you lay yourself open to serious business problems. What can you do to improve the way you communicate to people and listen to them? Let us admit right here and now that there are no slick tricks or quick gimmicks. This kind of talking and listening is a skill, and one that like any other skill comes with practice. Furthermore, if you are to improve in this skill you will need some feedback, some tool to check out how well you are doing. It is possible to go on some courses to get you started. If you can get two or three of your colleagues to work with you and form a little self-help group, this will help you to improve much faster. However, if you feel you can't do either of these things, it is still possible to improve, but it is not easy.

You may wonder why we have described talking and listening as one skill rather than two. Whilst it is true to say that you can talk and not listen or vice versa, the most effective communication is generally a two-way one. This is because people hear, understand and remember when they respond to what they hear. Two-way conversation can be a good way of keeping a check on that response and maintaining it. However, people sometimes get into conversations where they talk alternately, but when you break it down you find that there is very little connection between the ideas expressed by the two speakers. It is as if each one is giving a series of little speeches, interrupted by the other person doing the same. At the end of such a conversation it is likely that each has heard very little of what the other has said. That is not what I call two-way conversation, but it often happens.

Be clear about this. The alternating type of non-communicating conversation I have described is not frivolous. Quite the contrary, it generally occurs when both people are really serious. Each person is talking about something really important to him – or her. If you find yourself in such a conversation, what can you do? The common reactions are to continue as a kind of self-indulgence, hoping that some of your points get through, or to try to wrench the other person off his line of thought on to yours – especially if you're the boss. You will probably find it more productive in the long run to move on to the other person's track and find out what's bugging him or her. Once that has been brought out into the open and some decision taken (even if it's a decision not to act, or to defer the matter) you are generally in a better position to get your point across. This means you transform the conversation into two sequential two-way exchanges instead of a pattern of alternating soliloquies.

Were you heard?

Let's suppose you want to make a start on improving your skill on your own. Think back over the last week or so. Can you identify any specific incidents where you were misunderstood, or where you felt that someone who spoke to you looked frustrated and disappointed because you had not understood them. Write down a little note about incidents of the first kind on a sheet of paper ruled up and headed as in Figure 13:

- Who was it who misunderstood you?
- What was it about?

Figure 13 *Analysing misunderstanding*

Subject of the misunderstanding?

Who did you misunderstand?

What were the circumstances?

How can you avoid a recurrence?

Now think about the circumstances:

- How did you tell him or her?
- Are you sure they heard you properly in the first place – or was it in a noisy workshop?
- Are you sure they were concentrating on what you had to say, or were they trying to tell you about some problem they had, or trying to deal with some other matter at the same time, interjecting peremptory responses to you with comments into the telephone they were holding at the time?
- Was the order or message somewhat technical?
- Was it rather complicated to absorb?
- Did you get them to repeat back to you the essential points?
- Did you – or the other person – jot the key points down on a sheet of paper? (People remember visual images much better than oral ones in general.)

As you reflect on the circumstances and try to recognize what went wrong, ideas will begin to occur to you for the last section – how to put it right next time. One problem is more difficult to deal with – when the other person does understand in their minds what you have said, but somehow they feel they know best and so they do something different. For example, you may say to the foreman, this week we have to make twenty items of A, twenty items of B and ten of C, and I want your section to make, each day, four of A, four of B and two of C. Fine. He says he understands. On Thursday morning you go in and ask to see the C-items produced. But the foreman says that after you had gone he realized it would be more efficient to make items A on Monday and Tuesday, B on Wednesday and Thursday and C on Friday, so no items C have been made! Now if you had a good reason for your order, e.g. you wanted supplies of all three to be available on Thursday morning, the foreman did not know! He thought he understood you and did his best to meet your requirements as he understood them. Is the lesson clear? In such a case – and incidents of this kind abound – you have two choices. You either expect blind obedience 'to the letter' of your orders – a policy that will only work in certain circumstances – or you should make it clear to people why you want things done in a certain way.

Suppose you can't think of any recent examples where you have been misunderstood. Then watch out for the next time it happens and carry out a kind of inquest.

Did you hear?

Now let us look at the other side of the coin. Consider a recent incident where it seems you misunderstood someone. Rule up a sheet of paper as in Figure 14:

- What was it about?
- When one of your people comes to you with a problem what is your reaction?

There are a number of ways you can respond. There is no consistently 'right' way, indeed quite the reverse. If you always respond in the same way you are virtually certain to be wrong quite often. Perhaps the word *wrong* is not the best word to use, but *unhelpful* might be pretty near the mark. Before we proceed with the rest of Figure 14 let's pause to consider alternative ways to respond.

Suppose one of your people comes along to say that some of the items produced on the previous day are defective, and that he does not know whether to scrap them, to try to salvage them by some re-work, or to let them go through although they are a bit substandard. One response would be to instantly seize the initiative and deliver an immediate decisive response. 'Scrap them' or 'let them through'. You may consider that you heard and understood the message and that your response was entirely appropriate. But was it? The likelihood is that what the foreman wanted was not a decision, but rather **some guidance on how to decide**. The next time he has such a problem he will either run to you with it or do it by rule of thumb – if he thought that that was how you decided. In effect you are saying much more to him than 'scrap them' or 'let them through'. Furthermore you probably heard less than what he meant and he heard more than you meant to say.

Snatching away problems and solving them in this way does a lot for your ego and it keeps the thing moving along at that point, but it

Figure 14 *Analysing misunderstanding*

Subject of the misunderstanding?

Who misunderstood you?

What were the circumstances?

How can you avoid a recurrence?

hardly develops the foreman's ability to make decisions or improves his job satisfaction. Do it occasionally when you're busy by all means, but at some point you should perhaps take time out to help your foreman think through the issues involved, and the pros and cons of different solutions. Then he will make good decisions and save you work. This means investing time in people so you can get it back – with interest – later. In the jargon its called 'coaching'. There are two ways to do this. One 'coaching' response to the foreman is to ask him a barrage of questions. How bad is the defect? What will it cost to put right? What will it cost to the firm if we scrap them? Have you made sure the machine is properly set today? Once again this could be helpful. It will cause the foreman to think through a lot of the issues involved. It will sharpen his analytical powers – provided he is up to answering these questions. A hard pounding with questions can be off-putting to some folk and make them feel inadequate. If you help him think through the answers to a decision, he'll learn a great deal. Of course, if you snatch all the answers and decide yourself, we are back to square one.

Another approach is to try to help the foreman to solve the problem himself, and to keep 'ownership' of it as we say. In other words you might say 'Let's see now, what do you think we ought to do? What are the issues involved? Tell me what you think would happen if we tried each of your three ideas?'. This will take longer than your snap decision, and longer than the probing questioning approach. If time is really short, these may be best in the short run. If you have the time, this slower approach, getting the person concerned to think up all the issues and outcomes will probably give you a better decision more often, and it is much more likely to help your foreman to improve his powers of analysis and decision making.

The foreman's problem we've been looking at is technical, and not overloaded, generally, with a lot of emotion. Some problems, however, are much deeper into the realms of feelings. Suppose your office supervisor comes in one day and says 'I don't seem to be able to get through to that new boy who joined us three weeks ago. I have shown him how to deal with the morning mail a dozen times and still he gets it wrong. I don't feel as if I'm getting anywhere with him'. How might you respond to that? You might snatch the problem away and deal with it. 'Send him into me and I'll soon sort it out'. You might ask a barrage of questions. 'Have you tried this? Have you done that? How long has this been going on?' You might try to share the problem. 'Tell me all about it and let's see if we can find a solution.' The first alternative would probably be a disaster. You can't win that way. If you do tell the lad how to do it and he succeeds every day thereafter you have undermined both the confidence and the authority of the supervisor and made her job more difficult. Far from solving her problem, you have created a bigger one. If you had listened carefully, the problem was not that the lad was not doing the job properly, it was that she had difficulty communicating with him. Far from helping with her problem, the snatching-away method has amplified the difficulty.

The barrage of questions is not much better in this case. When feelings are aroused most people become defensive when confronted by a series of hard-hitting questions. Especially when they start with a sense of failure. It usually does nothing to improve their confidence. Indeed, the likelihood is that the mail-sorting is a symptom or an example of the problem and not the key to the problem at all. Probing the symptom may not lead to the root of the trouble which may lie elsewhere. You may think you have understood the situation, and you put your own interpretation on it. 'You don't treat him properly. Treat him like an adult. Be more forthright. Give him a good ticking off.' This might work if you are the supervisor, but it's not always easy for people to take advice like that, particularly if it's not the way they usually work. The likelihood is that the supervisor will listen politely, utter some grudging agreement and thanks and shuffle out of your office frustrated and disappointed. You have not listened, and you have come up with what seem to be half-baked non-solutions.

What's left? Perhaps the only real solution is to help the supervisor to think through a solution of her own. That means that you must not try to solve the 'symptom' yourself, nor to guess what lies behind it, or to probe in the areas where you think the solution might lie. One way to start – if you re-read the supervisor's statement – is where she left off. 'You feel you are not getting anywhere with this new lad.' Such a response leaves the supervisor with the problem, and enables her to open it up in her own way. If you allow someone to explore the problem in their own way like this you can help them to see it in perspective. When you consider that the main points come out, you might then begin to ask more pointed questions like 'What do you think you might do about it?' and later still, perhaps, 'Is there anything you feel I can do to help?'. You must recognize that you are treading on dangerous ground, and great care and sensitivity is needed to deal with people – both men and women – who have problems that involve their feelings. But you won't make much progress in the long run by ignoring the way people feel, because it will affect their personal relationships with you and the other people in the firm, and their motivation and effectiveness.

Now let's get back to Figure 14. Write down the circumstances of the misunderstanding, and how you responded. In the last section see if you can think of ways to prevent a recurrence of that type of problem. Do remember that there is no right or wrong response, but rather ones which are more or less helpful in given situations. Making an appropriate response comes with practice and getting better at sensing what kind of a problem you're dealing with. It comes from being able to recognize the silent signals people give you when they don't understand, or don't really believe you, or don't really agree or don't feel that you are really listening. There is generally no time to sit down and analyse the situation to determine the right response. It must come intuitively, as it were, and be the result of improving your personal skill.

Reviewing the situation Earlier we spoke about an inquest on incidents where misunderstandings occurred. Now and then such a review can be very helpful. There is a most important thing to remember, however. Do not make this into a witch-hunt. The idea should be to look for ways to improve communications, not to look for someone to blame. If people know you are looking for a culprit, everyone becomes defensive. This has two damaging effects. First of all, it makes it harder to get at the truth. Secondly, it sets people against each other and impedes effective collaboration.

When you have had a conversation with someone it is sometimes useful to sit down afterwards for five or ten minutes and to reflect on what took place. Try to recall the key points in the conversation and your reaction, and the other person's as each new idea unfolded. At first you may find this review difficult, but as you get more practice you will find it is a good way to get pointers for improvement. You might ask yourself questions like:

- Did I say the things I wanted to say. Do I think I let the other person have his say, or did I interrupt him at a key point and possibly lose something?
- Am I sure he really understood what I said?
- Am I confident he will do what I ask in the way I want it done?
- Did I give him the chance to ask questions and to put forward ideas?
- Did I pour cold water on everything he said, or encourage him to set out his ideas, even if I could not agree in the end?

If you had been recording the conversation in any way you would soon see how true are your impressions of the interview. Your memory is not likely to be very accurate, but it's a start.

People in groups and meetings

So far we have been talking about the one-to-one situation – a normal everyday occurrence which one hardly thinks about. It is worth spending some time on what happens when a group of people (three to ten, say) get together for a business meeting. If you have such meetings and can get your colleagues to collaborate, there are some useful, simple tools about that can be used to help groups of people to work together more effectively. They work, in effect, by holding up 'mirrors' so that you can all see what is going on. You can then make sensible decisions yourself on how to do better. (Once again there are courses and consultants which can be very helpful in these areas.)

These tools are based on the fact that when a group of people get together to achieve a task, a process of interaction between the people is necessary for the task to be achieved efficiently and effectively. If you call a meeting, the first thing to do is to be sure you know why you have called it and what you can expect to get out of it. Then you ought to consider this from the viewpoint of those who you invite. Why should they come? Because you are the boss? That's a good enough reason, but they will soon get fed up if they can't see some real purpose in the meeting which concerns them.

Briefings I suppose one of the simplest reasons for calling a meeting is so that you can, for example, tell your senior group about some new development. In your mind you think of yourself saying a few words and sending them away. But they may want to ask questions, or raise matters which have nothing to do with the issue you wish to pronounce upon. How will you handle that in a way that maintains the motivation of your people and their confidence in you? Incidentally, it is generally better not to provide chairs if you intend to have a brief meeting to give information. Chairs encourage people to settle down and be expansive, especially if they are not to be involved in problem-solving or decision-making.

Reviewing progress Suppose you want a meeting to review progress and to discuss and decide upon the ongoing problems:

- Do have a simple agenda or prescribed order; without it the discussion will probably dodge about and waste everybody's time.
- Don't let people bore the group by reading out a lot of facts and figures that could have been photocopied and handed round.
- Expect people to come to the point quickly.
- Don't, however, ignore the folk who can't jump into conversations quickly. They are often people who have something very valuable to say. Make sure they can get a word in.

Brainstorming meetings Of course, you may have a difficult problem which, it seems, cannot be solved by logic or negotiation. It needs a creative solution. The first two kinds of meeting are not much use here. People can't be constrained by rigid agendas and timetables if you want them to think up original ideas. There are several techniques for encouraging creativity. Probably the simplest and best-known is brainstorming. Don't run away with the idea that brainstorming is just letting everybody talk at once. It is not. There is a sequence of events which must be properly controlled. In essence having made sure you all understand the problem, you begin by 'opening up' the discussion. Ask people to contribute ideas. Write them down, preferably in a flip-chart where everyone can see them. Just jot them down as headings. Don't – at this stage – allow any explanation of the ideas or any questions to be asked. Just get the ideas flowing, however crazy they may seem. When the flow dries up, go through the lists again and ask each person to explain the idea(s) he or she contributed. Once again do not allow criticism of the idea, but you may permit questions designed to ensure that everybody understands what is being proposed. The next stage is where you start to take each other apart and select the few that really seem to have promise. Finally you take these ideas and turn them into concrete plans.

In the preceding paragraphs we have explored just three types of meeting. They are very different, and the process of interaction will be very different in each case. You can, of course, have a meeting in which all three tasks have a place, but then the style and pace of the meeting should change with the task. As we have seen before, there is not a right and a wrong way to run a meeting, but there is an appropriate way if you want effectiveness.

Handling meetings How can you get a handle on the process? A simple way is unobtrusively to note how many times each person speaks. Even more sophisticated is to note how long each person speaks. For example in the 'information' type meeting it is likely that the boss talks most of the time. Fine. In the progress meeting one would expect the line managers each to have a share in the 'air-time'. How much time they take will depend on what needs to be reported and discussed. If you found week after week that one person hogged all the meeting you would have to consider whether this was a good use of time. The creative meeting is even more interesting. If you noted down the style of the meeting as it proceeded you should observe a lot of quick-fire contributions from everybody – or most people anyhow. Then as you move to explanations, criticisms and finally to the planning stage, contributions will become longer and more considered. If you notice someone is not contributing, ask yourself why. Is it because the matter does not concern them, or they need to know, but not to contribute ideas, or are they shy, bored, or are they upset by what someone else has said? What about someone who is not listening, or that person who is too busy composing his next little speech to care about what others are saying? Just as we found two people can talk without really communicating, a lot of this goes on at meetings. If it happens too much you and your team are wasting a lot of valuable time and probably getting mediocre decisions into the bargain.

How can you check this out? One way is to stop the business occasionally and ask one or two people if they are happy with the proposal or whatever, and then to follow this up by asking them what they understand by this decision and how it will affect them. You can also stop the business sometimes and say, 'Well is everybody satisfied that they have had their say and that this is the best solution?'. There are, of course, many more sophisticated tools, but as the busy manager of a small firm you are not likely to want them. The key question is, are people involved in the meeting, playing a useful part and getting something out of it? Is the meeting achieving something useful without wasting time? If you are feeling really ambitious, it may be worthwhile to actually analyse the kind of contribution people are making during meetings. A simple method is described in the Appendix.

Preparing an agenda If you want to run a meeting in a very business-like way, you should have an agenda, make sure everyone sticks to the point and at intervals you, as chairman, should summarize what the meeting has decided before moving on. You can be even more formal and ask someone to take notes and keep minutes. Minutes of meetings should be as short as possible, recording decisions and, perhaps, key arguments put forward. If you consider it wise to be that formal you can even get people to prepare papers which should be given to those who are expected to attend, along with the agenda, far enough ahead for them to read them. If you have technical matters to discuss, then previously distributed papers are vital. Even technical papers should be as brief as possible, provided always that all the essential data is presented. Documents which must be long should have a summary, say not more than fifty to a hundred words, pointing out the key issues and matters for decision. Do not impose a level of formality which is inconsistent with the style of your firm.

If you decide to have a regular meeting of your senior staff (say once a week or once a fortnight), **be careful it does not become a waste of time**. It is sometimes useful to work out the cost of a meeting, just in terms of the hourly costs of the people involved. It will give you a sense of what you should expect from it. For such regular meetings formal minutes are rarely justified, but a brief note of key points might be useful. Don't get into the habit of solemnly going through all the points that came up last week! That will make the meetings longer and longer and decreasingly cost-effective.

Sometimes a good way to conduct such meetings is to ask each person present to say quickly what he wants to talk about. Just the subject heading, no more. Then you can decide what will be dealt with, taking the important things first and leaving trivial matters until last. It is a good idea to hold such meetings at about 11 or 11.30 in the morning so that by 12.30 everybody is itching to get away for lunch.

Action Guidelines

1 How can you be sure that your instructions are properly understood?

2 How can you improve your own ability to grasp exactly what is being said to you?

3 If you intend to hold a meeting, what work will you do beforehand to prepare for it?

4 If you are holding a meeting, how will you deal with someone who talks too much? What will you do to encourage someone to talk when you think they are holding back, and have a useful contribution to make?

5 How can you ensure that decisions taken at meetings are acted upon?

10
How to Write to People

- Before you write to someone, make sure you know what you are trying to achieve, whether it is a letter, an internal note, or a circular.
- Are you sure you are writing to the right person or persons? Is your purpose clear?
- Is this the best way to proceed, or would the message be better conveyed by telephone or personal visit?
- Write simply. Read it over carefully to check that the person who will read it will quickly grasp the right message.
- Ask yourself how you would react to such a letter or note, and try to gauge how the other person will respond.
- Beware of provoking reactions that will frustrate your purpose, e.g. resentment or hostility.

Clarity and style

Some people write a lot of notes and letters, and find it easy to put pen to paper. Others feel it is irksome to put things in writing and tend to work mainly by word of mouth and to use the telephone a lot. If you find it very easy to string words together you may well be tempted to use too many words, thereby wasting not only your own time in preparing written documents, but also that of the people you hope will read them.

On the other hand, if you do not readily put things down on paper, your writing style may be somewhat stilted and inelegant. It does not always work out this way, but there is no doubt that many businessmen scarcely pause to consider just how effective they are when it comes to the written word. Because it is clear to the writer what he or she means, it is assumed that the message must be equally clear to the reader. It does not always follow, and whenever your letter or memorandum gives the wrong message, you have potentially damaged the business in some way.

There's no simple formula for writing good letters and notes, but by giving a little thought and time to this matter it is possible to avoid most of the pitfalls and to improve one's powers of communication and persuasion in writing. We shall first of all think about a number of typical situations and what is involved in writing a good letter or note. We shall use a checklist approach for this, and you may find it helpful to use the checklist as you compose one or two documents which you consider important – just to get the idea. It is clearly quite impracticable to use the checklist every time, but once you grasp the essentials you will probably find yourself mentally checking off one or two key points as you compose critical letters or whatever.

Once you have read this Unit you may also find it helpful to use the checklist to look at some of the letters or notes you have sent out recently. The checklist itself is given in Figure 15, but it will not make much sense until you have read what follows.

Let us consider some different kinds of letters or notes that a businessman might wish to send:

- You may want to write to your bank manager for a loan, or to a buyer from whom you hope to receive an order.
- You might want to leave some written instructions for the foreman when you have to leave the premises on urgent business, or to write a letter to a supplier who has let you down.
- You may feel you would like to sent a note to one of your people who has been off sick for several weeks.

These may be very different letters (indeed they should be!) but there are some basic questions we can consider which apply in every case.

Figure 15 *Letter-writing checklist*

Preparation

1 To whom is the letter addressed?
  - name(s)
  - job(s)
  - level of understanding
  - relationship to writer

2 Why is the letter written?
  - convey information?
  - produce action?
  - convey/induce emotion?

3 What is the precise message?
  - key information points?
  - key action points?
  - promise of follow-up?

4 What response do you want to get?
  - understanding?
  - on the record?
  - action?
  - empathy?

5 Getting it down
  - handwriting?
  - typewriter?
  - multiple copies?

Review

6 What response do you think your letter will actually produce?
7 Are you sure your message is quite clear and unambiguous?
8 Does it actually convey the message you intended?
9 Are there emotional overtones in the letter? Are these appropriate?
10 How would you react if you received a letter like that?

To whom?

Using the checklist, to whom is the letter addressed? If you know the person well – be it the bank manager, foreman or your employee – you may want to use his or her first name. But don't do it unless that is the way you would address the person face to face.

The job the person holds and the level of understanding they bring to the subject of the letter or note will help you decide how 'technical' you can be. The bank manager will know a lot about money, loans, interest rates and securities, but not much, perhaps, about your business and the Doppler DG9X machine you want to buy from Germany with the money you hope to borrow. He will be more interested to hear why you think the Doppler DG9X is a good investment, and how your firm will earn the extra cash through using it, i.e. that will pay off the loan – and how soon.

When you write to the foreman, on the other hand, he will know about the technicalities of your business and your note can be full of technical terms and abbreviations which he will recognize. If, however, you want him to do something for you which is outside the normal range of his duties and experience, you may need to spell out what you want done in more detail.

The relationship of the recipient to the writer is an important consideration. In business sometimes one person is asking for something, and the other person is often indifferent to the outcome. For example, when everybody is clamouring for loans, it does not matter much to the bank whether a loan goes to you, or to someone else – provided the bank considers the security is adequate. That puts you in the position of suppliant, and you are not in a position to 'drive a hard bargain'. Similarly if everyone wants to get supplies from the same source, you are in a weak position to demand rapid deliveries. Sometimes, of course, the roles are reversed and you may be in the strong position. The tone of your letter might reflect this in subtle ways, but it is rarely a good policy to push your advantage to the limit, or to admit to being in a very weak position.

Why write?

Let us consider why you are writing a letter, and not making a telephone call or a personal visit. If you are writing to the bank manager, for example, you will want your request for a loan to be on the file in the bank, and you will want to present a concise account of the precise facts as a basis for a discussion with him when you do visit him. Indeed he may have requested such information. In writing to your defaulting supplier, again you might want the incident to be down on paper in case it happens again and you want to take the matter further, e.g. write to a more senior person. Incidentally, if you do *not* want it on the record it may be better not to write a letter. The value of sending a letter to the supplier is in the opportunity to set out the facts as you see them, which gives him a chance to look into where things went wrong and how future problems can be avoided.

Information and action The written document is quite good at conveying straightforward information, if it's carefully prepared. But you may want more. You may want action to follow directly as the result of your note – as in the case of the foreman we cited above. In this case look at the request/command sentences and try to read them very literally. Have you assumed some knowledge, or that some accompanying action will be taken along with what you have written down? You may hope that the buyer will place an order in response to your letter. Have you made that quite clear? If your letter or note is long, it's a good idea to repeat the key point at the end, e.g. to the foreman 'Finally Joe, don't forget to load the paper into the Doppler machine so that we can make an early start on Friday' – or to the buyer 'I look forward to receiving your order for 10,000 steel generator cover bands'.

When you write to someone who is sick, however, the information you convey is generally incidental to the main purpose of expressing sympathy and conveying good wishes. These letters are essentially emotional in character. You may want to fill out the letter with some news about the firm or the people, to help the invalid feel he or she is still part of the team – 'We got that big order from Blenkinsop Mills' or 'Jane had her baby last week'. But essentially you want the individual concerned to realize that they are remembered and that you wish them a speedy recovery and return to the workplace. This will influence the words you use.

Choosing words

So much for the preliminaries. Now you must choose the words and compose the sentences, bearing in mind who is to read the letter, exactly what you want to convey and to result from your letter. How do you start? The level of familiarity in your opening can vary enormously according to how well you know the person, the purpose of the letter and the cultural norms of the group to which you and the other person belong. What do I mean? It is usual to begin letters 'Dear Mr Jackson', or 'Dear Ms Jones' these days, and to say 'Dear Sir or Madam' if you do not know the name of the person you are addressing. It is unwise to use first names unless you know the person well enough to do this in normal conversation, as it may be regarded as unduly familiar. You should be especially concerned about etiquette if you trade with overseas people. This is a matter for you to judge.

Some people find it hard to get started. If you are replying to a letter the trusted formula 'Thank you for your letter dated 17 July 1983...' is fine. You can warm it up a bit by inserting 'very much' or 'very much indeed' if you found the original particularly welcome, but the simple phrase is quite good. If your letter is the start of the correspondence you might begin with a word of explanation, e.g. 'I am writing to tell you about our new line in packing cases' or 'We met recently at the Golf Club and it occurred to me that you might be interested to learn more about my firm's products'. It's as well not to get into a request for a loan or an order until you have established some rapport in the letter and explained why you need a loan or feel worthy of an order. If you are really stuck, get out a sheet of paper and write down simply in your own words what you want to say. Then you can simply put these ideas into some order, string them together, smarten up the English and make sure the meaning is clear.

A short letter, to the point, is always acceptable. In general, use short sentences. The longer the sentences, the easier it is for people to lose the meaning. Once you have your rough ideas mapped out you should have little difficulty in breaking these down into short sharp sentences. Of course, there are occasions when, for technical reasons, the words and sentences are long. So be it – if you are sure it is really necessary. Try to avoid repeating the same words over and over again, especially in the same sentence. Of course, again this may be necessary for technical reasons, and occasionally for literary effect – although the latter should not be overdone in business letters.

Most business documents are typed, but the handwritten letter can be most effective (if it's legible), when you want to 'personalize' it – for example to congratulate someone, or to express sympathy or thanks for a kindness. Unless you type your own letters, the text must reach the typist. You can give the typist a handwritten text, or you can dictate it personally or use a dictating machine of some kind. If you decide to use a machine, you need training. The typist will want to know when to start and finish a sentence, how to spell names and so forth. Beware of dictating too much. It is very easy to be expansive talking into a machine as opposed to writing each word by hand. The fast flow of words may be useful if you are trying to write a racy novel, but it is not conducive to a concise, easily read letter or memorandum.

Circulars

We have assumed so far that you are writing to an individual. Suppose you are writing a circular letter, or a note to a number of your people? The same basic ideas apply, but here you are thinking of a group of people:

- Try to ensure that the least intelligent person and the least well informed will be able to understand it.
- Keep is as short and simple as possible. When people see a circular they are not inclined to wade through a lot of verbiage.
- Go for short paragraphs – not more than six to eight lines. The space between paragraphs will make the letter look less daunting to read.
- If you want to send the same letter to a lot of people, the modern word processor with a good 'typewriter' finish is ideal as they can be run off with different names and addresses on individual letters. A good quality photocopy is satisfactory, but expensive to personalize and it never looks quite right.

If some of these circulars go to people you know personally, a very brief handwritten note at the foot of the page helps to convey friendship even if the rest is duplicated, or obviously the product of a word processor.

Let's assume you have drafted the letter, but it is important and you want to be sure you have got it right:

- Look at the second part of Figure 15 – the Review section.
- Read through the letter.
- Ask yourself what response you think it is likely to produce.
- Is the message crystal clear, or could parts of the letter be misunderstood – or worse still deliberately misconstrued to your disadvantage?
- Does it actually convey the message you intended – in terms of information or request for action (or command).
- Are there emotional overtones, and are they appropriate? You may be angry with the supplier, but will it actually help your business if that spills over into your letter? Or would an unemotional letter that firmly demands better service in future be more productive?
- Then there's the acid test – what would you do if you received a letter like that? Of course, there's no guarantee that the other person will react similarly, but it may give you a clue on how to firm up a paragraph here and there, or to take the heat out of some criticism to make the letter more constructive.

From time to time you may want to prepare special documents, e.g. reports or sales material. It is difficult to go into detail since the purpose of the report and its destination will vary enormously, and the sales letter must be geared very closely to the particular market. It is as well for you and your senior staff to be clear about how to write down brief reports of events, e.g. machine breakdowns, or brief instructions on how to operate machines or comply with simple procedures. Such ability is of particular value if you have to write reports on accidents, or on disciplinary or grievance matters. The essential point here is to be methodical, to use simple words as far as possible, and short sentences.

The sales letter or circular must have an immediate impact if it is not to be discarded rapidly. You must decide – on the basis of your potential customers – whether the approach should be racy, punchy or the 'soft-sell'. The opening paragraph must say something arresting, and you must stress why people should buy your goods or services. Keep any mention of costs until later on, unless this is a key selling point. It is a good idea to get someone else to read through your draft before you launch into print. We all have a tendency to read what we wanted to say rather than what we have actually written, and to miss any oddities or double-meanings in the text.

Action Guidelines

1 What kind of instructions and information should be put in writing for your people, rather than relying only on word of mouth?

2 How can you ensure that your letters and notes are understandable to the intended reader and likely to achieve the desired effect?

3 How can you decide that a letter is necessary rather than, or in addition to, a telephone call?

4 How can you ensure that reports are of an adequate standard?

5 How can you improve your sales production material?

II
The Opposite Sex

- For the most part, men and women work very well together. But sometimes problems can arise.
- If a number of women report to a man, it is vital for him to treat each one with respect as a person. He must avoid any favouritism or any actions which can be misconstrued.
- If a number of men work for a woman, the key-word again is respect. She must endeavour to earn respect and to give due heed to the opinions of her subordinates.
- Managers, both men and women, must avoid any form of discrimination.

The difference

There are three aspects to this problem:

- Women who work for men.
- Men who work for women.
- Men and women working together for the same boss.

It is tempting to try to deal with the first two situations together and to say quite glibly throughout this section that 'he' includes 'she' and vice versa. This would be dishonest. The problems are similar up to a point, but by no means the same. As a matter of fact men and women are different, psychologically as well as physically. This is not to deny the movement towards equality of opportunity and so forth, but simply to point out that in real life, management situation differences must be recognized and dealt with, not swept aside.

These differences are more than a matter of appearances. Women are, in general, not as strong, physically, as men, although it must be pointed out quite forcefully that there a lot of physically strong women, and weak men! The number of physically demanding jobs – in terms of sheer strength – is no longer very great. There are plenty of modern aids to eliminate the need for brute strength. When it comes to stamina, women can normally hold their own in the work situation. This means that it is rarely justified to insist that a man does a particular job merely because of physical strength demands.

But this is not the real point at issue when it comes to a woman being supervised by a man – or vice versa. The differences that matter here are to do with the mind and with feelings. Whether it comes about by heredity or upbringing is not our concern here, but there can be little doubt that, in general, women tend to approach many problems and situations differently to men. If you are prepared to accept that different viewpoint, it can be an asset to the firm. By looking at problems in more than one way we can often come up with more imaginative solutions. If one of your people makes a suggestion which seems silly at first sight, do not be too quick to dismiss it. If you take the trouble to understand, you may find the germ of a good idea behind it. On the other hand, if these differences of perspective are not taken into account, they can give rise to misunderstandings and inefficiency.

Man in charge

If you, as a man, have a number of women reporting to you, what is the key to effective management? It can be summed up in a word – 'respect'. You must cultivate a person-to-person relationship with each one which is based on mutual respect and integrity. Respect each person as someone else's wife, mother or girl friend. Your job is to manage the production, not to get involved in their personal lives beyond the polite interest of a colleague at work. Resist any temptations to make improper advances. Don't forget that these may easily be regarded as taking unfair advantage of someone in your employment. It could easily be termed 'sexual harassment' and although it may only seem like a practical joke to you, others can take it very seriously indeed. If you are confronted with a female colleague or member of your staff who is distressed, you must be careful as you express sympathy and offer support, that you maintain, as it were, a discreet distance. It is all to easy, on such occasions, for an act of sympathy to be misconstrued. The more genuine sympathy you feel for the person, the more careful you must be.

The respect you have for your staff must be demonstrated in scrupulous fairness in your dealings. You must not have 'favourites' who get all the perks, all the cushy jobs and all the information before anybody else. Of course, if the individual concerned is your secretary, your deputy or your personal assistant, they will inevitably have a special working relationship with you, but even this must not be allowed to get out of hand. It is not unknown for the secretary to rule the roost by regulating the flow of information and people who get to the boss, especially if the latter is shut in an office all the time. You must not allow this to happen. Make sure you see all your key people personally and often. They must be able to get to see you.

You must also avoid at all costs giving the impression that one particular lady has some kind of power over you. (Or man, for that matter!) You will notice that I have deliberately used the word 'impression'. How things look to people is just as important as how things are in reality. Needless to say, you must carefully reject any improper advances you yourself receive.

Woman in charge

Now suppose you are a woman and you have a number of men working for you. Once again the key-word is respect. There is an additional emphasis here, however, as some men might feel threatened by the thought of working for a woman. This feeling is less common, but it has not disappeared. How can you, as a woman, gain the confidence and support of men in your business endeavours. Since we are concerned with pragmatism rather than idealism, the truth is you have got to demonstrate unequivocally that you know what you are about and that, having listened carefully to advice, you can make up your mind. This is not such a problem for a male boss, as he is expected to know his job. If he does not, he is found out eventually and his staff will lose confidence in him. In today's society a woman will often find that to manage men well she must start with a conscious effort to establish credibility, firmness and fairness. Once these qualities have been demonstrated, most men will quite happily work for a woman.

A woman who wants to manage men effectively should respect them. Both men and women become disheartened or angry if they are belittled by someone – especially if others are present. If a woman manager rides rough-shod over the men who work for her, the efficiency of her team is unlikely to last for long. This is not a question of being soft, giving in or feeding the male ego. It means accepting the subordinate's views as valid, even when it is necessary to overrule him. This question of helping people keep their self-respect has been dealt with in earlier Units, but it is especially pertinent in this area. It is scarcely necessary to say that you should avoid making – or receiving – improper advances.

Discrimination

The *Equal Pay Act, 1970*, was designed to eliminate discrimination between men and women in matters concerning their employment, e.g. pay, overtime, holidays, sick leave and so forth. Its provisions apply to even the smallest of firms. A woman must not be employed on less favourable terms and conditions than a man if she is doing the same or broadly similar work. The *Sex Discrimination Act, 1975*, makes it unlawful for any employer to discriminate against a woman (or a man) in employment matters on the grounds of her (or his) sex, and its provisions are more widespread than the 1970 Act. Before you advertise any job or engage any staff you must make sure you comply with this Act (and other relevant laws and regulations). We shall deal with recruitment and selection in general in Unit 15, but here it is important to stress that, in general, jobs should be open to both men and women and that the pay and conditions offered to a woman should be the same as for a man. There are one or two exceptions, e.g. in respect of retirement age and pension schemes, and special privileges in connection with pregnancy or childbirth. The Act does not in general apply to very small firms employing less than six people.

As an employer you must ensure that your staff do not discriminate in these matters as well. You must be particularly careful about advertisements. There are a very limited number of instances where being a man (or a woman) is a genuine occupational qualification for a job, e.g. considerations of decency or privacy. If a firm has six or more partners it is also unlawful to discriminate against a woman when taking on a further partner.

Working together

It is quite possible that two members of your staff may be mutually attracted to one another. This is not a treatise on morality, and if the relationship does not affect the business in any way it should not be your concern. You may be personally involved by being attracted to someone in the firm, and find that your feelings are reciprocated. As far as the business is concerned, however, there are two extremely important issues here. In the first place, amorous activities must not be tolerated in the workplace. If people want to hold hands and gaze into each others' eyes, let them find somewhere else to do it and their own time to do it in. Such actions not only reduce the output of the people concerned, it provides unwarranted distractions for other workers.

Secondly, the existence of such relationships must not interfere with the fairness and effectiveness of management. This can easily happen if one of the people concerned reports to the other. For example, if a male supervisor forms a liaison with one of the women in the work group for which he is responsible, or the boss forms an attachment to his secretary. These things happen. The obvious solution of separating the two people in the work situation may not be a realistic option. Let us consider the problem a little more deeply and get some ideas on how to handle it.

Take the supervisor example first. He might well be tempted to give his friend special favours at work. He might tell her what is going on in senior staff discussions so that she knows these things before other members of the team. Such occurrences may not seem important to the supervisor and they may not even be conscious decisions, but they provide the seeds of discontent. The boss must make sure these special favours and information leaks do not occur.

What about the secretary? When the boss gets busy he sometimes hides behind his secretary, who then acts as a kind of gatekeeper, letting people in to see the boss, and sorting out what information he receives. That gives the secretary a lot of power. In the short run, if there is an emergency, and if the secretary is reliable and sensible, it might work. In any other circumstances it will probably be a disaster. The boss must make time to see them when they need to do so. The problem is compounded if the boss forms an amorous liaison with his secretary. What supervisor will go to the boss and tell him his secretary is behaving badly – if he knows the secretary is the boss's lover? This is a question of business efficiency, not morality.

Action Guidelines

1 Are all your employees treated with respect – both men and women?

2 Are all your people treated with equal fairness, as between men and women, and as between different men and different women?

3 Does your company comply with the *Equal Pay Act, 1970*?

4 Does your company come within the scope of the *Sex Discrimination Act, 1975*? Do you comply with its provisions as far as they affect you?

5 Are there any relationships between men and women which interfere with the efficiency and effectiveness of your enterprise? How will you deal with these if they arise?

12
Coping with Young People

- Young people are not that different from older people.
- They are generally quite thoughtful and want to know the reasons for things – including the rules of the firm.
- They are not likely to go on being put upon for very long or to accept orders or rules they do not understand.
- Most young people want to do a worthwhile job, and if you are prepared to take a little trouble to explain things, they will respond with enthusiasm.
- Be careful not to stereotype young people. They are all different, and you can't really tell very much from their clothes or haircuts.

What's new?

What is so different about young people that we have to consider them separately? Well, underneath they are not so different from older people, but there are two things which have made a difference which any sensible employer will take into account – education and unemployment.

Why is it that some adults get on well with young people and are able to get them working enthusiastically, whereas others seem to cause so much aggravation? Is there a way to be better at dealing with younger people?

A little understanding will help, but what is needed is not so much psychoanalysis as common sense.

In simple terms, young people have been educated and brought up to expect a good life and a voice in their affairs. By and large they are unwilling to give blind obedience to anyone and are particularly sensitive to being pushed around or given a raw deal. The prospect of not getting a job leads to anger or depression and if the period of unemployment is prolonged then the young person concerned may not have acquired the normal skills and attitudes associated with productive endeavour – give and take, co-operating with others, working to a schedule and at a fair pace and so forth.

But just as no two adults are really alike, as we saw earlier, so it is wrong to stereotype young people too closely. Most of them want a job and to do a decent day's work for a decent day's pay. Many of them do not look much further ahead than that. The young people who succeed best at work are those who show an interest in the job and the company, who ask questions and recognize early on that people generally do better at work when they co-operate and each play their part. They come to realize that other people suffer when they do not behave responsibly, for example by turning up late or skimping a job. So often they have got used to the idea that arriving late or doing poor work is a personal matter which does not affect anyone else but themselves (and the attitude of the teacher).

This idea of belonging to a work-group and having a sense of loyalty to it is more important than many people imagine. It may not seem to have much to do with competence to do a job, but in fact it generally does make a difference to how well jobs get done.

Patience These ideas may give you some clues on how to deal with young people. Just as it is foolish to treat adults like children, so it is equally unproductive to be patronizing to young people. You can give information, training and working instructions to young people without talking down to them. Naturally you must be careful to use words and phrases which they can understand, and also check out from time to time that they have really grasped the message. You will also need to be patient if the individual concerned misunderstands or forgets part of what you have said. Some young people will be nervous at first, and others may be anxious to make a start and to make a good impression. In either case they are prone to miss part of what is said to them. Many misunderstandings or lacks of communication in conversations with young people arise from these attitude problems rather than any lack of intelligence on the part of the young people concerned.

Expectations Another key factor in dealing with young people is what you expect of them. If you expect them to be irresponsible and disruptive, you may, without thinking, actually reinforce any disruptive tendencies they may have. On the other hand, if you expect them to behave reasonably and responsibly, most young people will react positively to this and try to live up to your expectations – provided these expectations are themselves reasonable. It is really a question of being positive and pitching your expectations at a reasonable level. On matters of attitude to timekeeping, relations with other people, attitude to the job and so forth you can be very positive. When it comes to actual performance, it may take a while before this comes up to scratch, but with clear instructions, sound working conditions, support from fellow workers and encouragement from you, it will happen.

Positive help

Take a look at Figure 16. This summarizes some areas where you can take positive action to get the best working relationship with the young people in your firm. We shall deal with recruitment, selection and induction later, so here we shall assume the young person is already working in your company.

The basic information First of all, are you sure the young person is clear, even about all the simple things – hours of work, break times, where to hang up his coat, the names and jobs of all the people around and so forth? These things matter to young people, and not to know about them, and perhaps to do something wrong in ignorance, can be very worrying. When someone joins the firm – adult or young person – do you make sure that everyone who should be informed is told about it? Unannounced newcomers can seem a threat to mature adults. How much more so to insecure young people. It does not take much time to keep people informed, but it all adds up to treating them as adults (albeit young adults) and forms part of the pattern of support which does not cost much money, but can give solid returns.

Who gives this information? Some of it will be written down, but much of this is done by word of mouth. You may do it yourself or get the supervisors to do it. You may find it helpful to get a fellow

Figure 16 *Helping young people at work*

Basic information	• Who tells them? • Have you got a checklist? Does it cover, for example, cloakrooms, ensure hours of work are understood, where to eat, where to read fire instructions, safety instructions, first aid box, names and jobs of people around? (See also Unit 19.)
The work group	• Alongside a skilled worker? • Some knowledge of the work of other team members? • A chance to do some of the other jobs in due course?
Job instruction	• Clear instructions and demonstrations? • Encourage questions? • Check of understanding? • Quality consciousness?
Timekeeping	• Responsibility to group? • Travel problems? • Flexible starting times?
Versatility	• Attitude of mind? • Train for several tasks? • Helping others out?
People relationships	• The support of the group? • Fairness and firmness? • A sense of achievement?

worker, someone who will work with or near the young person concerned, to pass on a lot of this information. You or the supervisor can check out later that the youngster has got all the information straight.

Mixed age groups Don't forget that many young people are not used to working in a mixed age group. They are used to being taught by older people. Now they have to become accustomed to doing a job alongside someone who may be twenty, thirty or forty years older than themselves. There is no need to make too much of this, however, as young people tend to respond well to older people who know how to do their jobs well. If you have some really good workers who have some sympathy with young people, then you could be helping both by putting them alongside each other – skilled worker with young newcomer. Conversely, if you have a sloppy worker, or someone who seems to do as little as possible, it's a bad start for a youngster to be put alongside such a person. Do not be surprised – if you take this action – to find that the young person acquires the lazy ways of his or her mentor.

Loyalty How about this group loyalty idea? How can this be encouraged? The way to go about this is to help the young person to see how his or her work fits into the overall pattern. It is not very inspiring to be told that you must get on with your own job and mind your own business if you ask where the half-finished product you have to work on has come from, or what will happen to it when you have finished. Just to know how some simple task fits into the overall pattern in a small office or manufacturing plant, can help to make the boredom of repetition more bearable.

Broadening experience If, when the young person has mastered the task, he or she can be moved on to another part of the overall job for a change and to get wider experience, that is all to the good. Whereas many older people are content to do a routine repetitive job, provided they can chat with their workmakes, young people often need the stimulus of an element of variety. Indeed, with modern technology many of these repetitive jobs are disappearing and the need is for versatile workers who are ready to tackle a variety of jobs. You can make such a move a kind of reward for doing a sound job in the first assignment. Moving about in different jobs helps to reinforce this idea of the work group, as the individual begins to understand the contribution each person makes to the final product or service provided.

Job instruction We must now consider item 3 in Figure 16, job instruction. If you are used to dealing with adults, you will notice there are some differences when you come to instruct school-leavers. Adults tend to rely a lot on their experiences and to draw analogies as they listen to you and observe your demonstration of the work to be done. They have got used to finding out a lot of things for themselves, keeping their eyes open and asking their workmates. Generally speaking they are not afraid to ask questions if they are unsure about what is required.

Young people, on the other hand, have been accustomed to accept information and instruction more positively. They expect to be told clearly and unequivocally what to do. They have not been encouraged to seek help from classmates, or to use their experiences as a resource for learning. They are more accustomed to dealing with parts of a problem (by academic subject) rather than with the totality of an operation or experience. You will, therefore, have to ensure that your instructions are clear, that in your demonstration you try to pick out the points which, although second nature to you, are by no means obvious to the teenager. You will need to encourage the young person to ask questions, for example by patiently responding to them and ensuring that every query is seriously dealt with.

Building up confidence

In spite of what was said about the value of new challenges, many young people may be hesitant to try a new job or task. In part this is undoubtedly fear of failure and being made to look a fool. Whereas this does not worry young children, teenagers are often particularly concerned about this. You need, therefore, to do all you can to help them to succeed quickly. Nothing builds confidence quicker than a few solid – although modest – achievements. On the other hand, if you destroy someone's confidence by giving them tasks which are very difficult and where they fail frequently, it is not easy to pull back from this. Rebuilding confidence is much harder than simply building it up.

In some jobs there is a need for speed. Here again the rate at which you expect young people to speed up should be within their ability range, and yet pushing them just a little. Do not push them so hard that the reject rate rises too fast. That's not good for business and it's no way to train up people for a future in your firm.

A particular area where attention is needed is to do with quality. Some youngsters recognize fairly quickly that every single product must be satisfactory, but with some others the importance of consistent good quality does not seem to register. If you have young people who do not give adequate attention to quality, why not collect some poor quality items, show them to the young people and have a little chat about it – perhaps with one or two older workers. Ask them to think about how much this or that fault matters to the client, and follow up by saying something about what effect reject items have on the viability of the firm.

Timekeeping

What about timekeeping? If one of your young people is persistently late, try to consider why this might occur before you tackle the young person. If it is a question of his or her attitude, then an appeal to the group loyalty idea might be helpful. On the other hand the individual might have problems of a different kind. Whereas adults control the domestic scene by deciding when the household wakes up and has breakfast, for example, the teenager probably falls in with whatever domestic arrangements prevail. He or she may depend on a lift from a neighbour. There may be a very poor bus service. In such cases what is needed is not a telling-off and a stiff warning, but perhaps a problem-solving chat. 'Johnny, you seem to have problems getting in on time. What do you think can be done about this? If there is an hourly bus that gets the teenager in five minutes late, you might think about moving his hours of work by five minutes. A little give and take on a thing like this could go a long way, even if a lot of the other workers ask for the same privilege!

In small firms it is often necessary for people to 'muck-in' and help each other out. This means that they need to know something about each other's jobs and to cope with the more urgent tasks for people who are away. This element of versatility should not be denied to the youngster who proves himself or herself in the job. Versatility is as much an attitude of mind as a range of skills and knowledge, and it needs to be incalcated from day one. 'You will start by doing this job, but if you make a fair show of it we shall want you to try your hand at a variety of tasks over the next year or so.'

Relating to older workers

Once or twice we have hinted at the role of other workers and the way they can help or hinder the young person. It is not a bad idea to prepare them to receive the youngster and to seek their co-operation in helping to smooth the entry into the workplace. Like adults, young people vary a lot in the way they relate to people. Some are shy and retiring, some outgoing and chatty, some belligerent and distinctly difficult to get along with. Young people who behave like the first two groups rarely pose serious problems, and if they are excessively shy or very talkative you can usually deal with this by common sense. Encourage the shy one to ask a few questions by emphasizing the importance of a proper understanding of the firm and the job. Move the chatterbox away from a ready listener!

What about the aggressive person? As we have discussed earlier, aggression is often the product of fear. The individual feels inadequate, or oppressed, or isolated or in danger of being cheated or belittled. If this is true – as it is for many young people – then you may be able to cope simply by putting the individual in a supporting work group, encouraging some modest achievement, and by demonstrating that honest work is fairly rewarded and that you regard the person as an emerging adult who should be treated with dignity and respect. Don't expect sudden conversions, but you will often find that such young people make excellent, energetic workers once these hang-ups have been worked through.

Don't indulge in amateur psychiatry or make any special allowances or indulgences for belligerent young people. Some of them need the firm, fair hand of someone in charge to give them a sense of where they are in the scheme of things. If you are indecisive there's nothing for them to hold on to, as it were. You may, unfortunately, be unable to help some young people who have got very big chips on their shoulders. That's not your job if you are running a business.

Youth Training Scheme (YTS) The Youth Training Scheme, introduced by the Manpower Services Commission, is probably here to stay. Consider carefully whether you can accept a youngster for on-the-job training and work experience – perhaps in collaboration with a local YTS Managing Agent.

Action Guidelines

1 Consider how you can obtain an active commitment from young people during their first few months in your firm.

2 Consider the young people who are working for you. In what ways are they different from mature adults and how can you take account of this in the way you manage them?

3 Consider how you will select young people when you next have some vacancies. What sort of induction and training will you provide?

4 Should you have disciplinary methods which are different for young people? In what way?

13
Employing Disabled People

- Disabled people make good employees.
- Do your utmost to help any of your own people who become disabled.
- Consider filling your next vacancy with a disabled person.
- Modifications to plant and premises are probably not that difficult, and help is often available.

Loyal workers

Disabled people generally make very good employees. They are, typically, hardworking, loyal and good timekeepers. Nevertheless it is a sad fact that many people are disabled, and furthermore disabled people find it harder to get jobs than able-bodied people. One thing to remember is that disablement can take many forms. We think automatically of people who are unable to walk, but people who have defective hearing or sight, and people without the full use of their arms and hands are also 'disabled', and may need employment.

If one of your people is unfortunate enough to become disabled – through an accident or illness – you will want to take them back into the firm, but you will then have to face employing someone with a disability. Do your utmost to retain that person and do not be put off too easily by the difficulties which seem to be in the way. The Government – currently through the Manpower Services Commission – offers a range of services to disabled people and employers and you should get in touch with the local office, with the Disablement Resettlement Officer, who can give you advice and tell you what help is available. You can usually get expert medical and technical advice about whether the individual will be able to return to his or her former job, or whether there is another range of tasks to be done in your organization which the individual can perform. Be prepared to think more broadly than the existing range of jobs. It might be possible to rearrange the tasks into a new set of jobs, one of which could be done by the disabled person.

If the individual needs help in overcoming the limitations imposed by the disability, or a period of assessment to find out what work is most suitable, a course at an Employment Rehabilitation Centre might prove helpful. If the person needs to be trained up to do new tasks, the MSC may help by arranging a training course at a Skillcentre or elsewhere. The individual would receive allowances during such courses. The likelihood is that fellow workers will welcome the disabled person back and do all in their power to help with the adjustment back into working life.

The action of taking someone back after a long illness or an accident, especially when disablement has occurred, is not merely an act of kindness, it is generally sound business. Not only have you retained the services of someone who knows about the firm and can fit in readily into its ways, but you will help other workers to respect you and to feel more loyal to the firm. Don't forget that taking on someone new is often expensive in terms of recruitment and training costs.

Filling a vacancy

The next time you have a vacancy to fill, spare a moment to consider the following points and whether the job might be done by a disabled person:

- You may be worried about the risk that the person might fall ill again, or be unable to do the job, or require special facilities or take a long time to train up to be effective. In all these areas help can be obtained from the Government or one of its agencies, e.g. the Manpower Services Commission, Health and Safety Commission, National Council on Employment of Disabled People. You can generally get expert advice on medical, psychological and technical matters to help you assess whether a job is likely to be suitable for a particular disabled person.

- You may be able to have someone for some weeks on a 'job rehearsal', with an allowance being paid by the Government, to see how the person is likely to shape up on the job.
- You may be able to get help with training for the disabled person as well. It is difficult to be specific as the rules for such aids change from time to time, but since this is an ongoing problem it is worth finding out what help is currently available.

If you are thinking in terms of a school-leaver, remember that a number of young people are handicapped. Here it is the local careers service who will give advice, put you in touch with suitable young people and probably arrange for an assessment training course as appropriate.

Once you have a disabled person in your employment it is important to give them the chance to develop their skills and to improve their position in the firm if they have the ability. We all have an unfortunate tendency to treat people who are hard of hearing, partially sighted or blind, or unable to walk, as if they are not ordinary people. They are ordinary people! They have the same hopes and fears as other people and we must treat them with respect, and as mature adults. (Unless they are teenagers! Then we should treat them like we treat ordinary teenagers.)

Equipment and premises

Quite often there is no need to make any alterations to the premises or equipment. There are, however, situations where a minor modification to equipment, to the arrangement of equipment or to the organization of the job can make a real difference by making it possible for the disabled employee to contribute to the enterprise as fully as other workers. The kinds of changes that have been made include:

- Minor rearrangements in the workplace so that an employee can sit down to do a job which was formerly done standing, or adapting the controls on a machine so that they can be worked by hand, instead of by foot, or vice versa.
- A jig can be redesigned to speed up a spot-welding operation when hand movements must be slower than before.
- A counterbalanced drawing board will help an employee with restricted arm movements.
- Braille can be incorporated in measuring devices and keyboards.
- Visual signals can be added to sound signals for deaf workers.
- The Post Office has a range of aids to help the partially sighted, hard of hearing and other disabled people to use the telephone.

If such alterations are costly, there may well be grants available to help, and technical advice is generally available. Some pieces of equipment can be loaned to see if they will help the person concerned, before you decide to buy them.

Another problem concerns the ability to get about, to get to the workplace, to get around inside the building and to the toilet. For most disabled people this is not a problem, but for some it is a very serious hindrance. A reserved car parking space may help in some cases. There is often financial help from the Government for those who find it difficult to get about.

As far as the workplace itself is concerned, steps and staircases are a problem. Short runs can often be overcome by ramps. In some cases doorways may need to be widened to allow wheelchairs to get through to the workplace, the toilets or the canteens. Don't forget the emergency exit routes as well. These items should be borne in mind when you need to make any alterations to your premises. If you propose to make alterations specifically to help disabled people, it is worth enquiring about a grant towards the cost.

You may feel that you have introduced an extra element of risk by employing a disabled person. Generally speaking, provided reasonable care is taken in matching the person to the job and that due attention is paid to hazards and exit routes, the increased risk is minimal. The Health and Safety Executive or the local Fire Authority will be happy to give you advice on specific problems.

Action Guidelines

1 Have you thought about employing a disabled person?

2 How do you set about finding someone suitable?

3 What sort of alterations will you need to make your premises, equipment or work organization?

4 Consider the implications for other members of your staff when you employ a disabled person. Can you give any advice to the people who will work closely with the disabled person?

5 What special training will you need to provide for the disabled person?

6 What sort of help can you expect from the authorities?

14
People and Technology

- Technology is only one aspect of change, but a very important one.
- Before installing new equipment you will need to be sure it will help the business, that you can afford it in the short run, and that your people will co-operate in making full use of it. If they do not, you will waste a lot of money.
- To gain the co-operation of your people, consider how it will affect each and every job, and the people involved. Get their views, and help them understand its effects.
- Train them to use it with confidence, and keep an eye on how things are going, especially at the early stages.

Aspects of change

There is nothing new about improving the way people work by introducing better tools. What is different about the current wave of new technology, particularly that based on microelectronics and the silicon chip, is the speed at which it is being developed and the profound changes it makes possible in virtually every aspect of our lives at home, at leisure, at work, and in all the other activities, e.g. shopping and medical matters, which occupy our time. Other technologies are also beginning to have an impact, e.g. lasers and biotechnology. It must be recognized, however, that the introduction of new tools, new technological equipment and consequently new working methods, are only one of the aspects of change which managers must master.

Many managers of small firms hesitate to introduce new technology in the 'office' side of the business or in the manufacturing and distribution side. The common reasons are fear of the unknown, a lack of cash or because they are not sure how the workforce will react. It is the last issue which we shall discuss in this Unit. As the manager of a small firm you must decide whether to invest in a particular piece of equipment for the workshop, the warehouse, the retail shop or the office. Let us assume that, purely on commercial grounds, you believe that the investment will bring an adequate return because it will increase the quality and/or quantity of goods or services your firm can produce in relation to staffing and other costs.

Generally speaking this will involve improving productivity, i.e. more output per person. Naturally your people will have a legitimate interest in such a decision for two distinct reasons. First of all, how does it affect their employment prospects in your firm? Secondly, how will it affect the work they will be required to do in the future? There are several aspects to this last question, for example will the work be congenial, satisfying, and within their competence, or will it become unpleasant, dangerous, demanding, boring and too difficult? These are very real issues for the people concerned and unless you deal with them in a sensible and sensitive manner you will precipitate real anxiety which will disrupt the effectiveness of your enterprise.

Before deciding

It is for you to decide at what stage you will discuss these matters with senior colleagues, your work people and, where appropriate, with employee representatives. In general the sooner the better. The more firmly your mind is made up and you are committed to a particular decision, the less open you are to sincere consultation. If you can 'float' ideas without being intensely committed to them, you will get better advice from your people at all levels. Of course most people will be hesitant about change at first, but given time to think it over and to get used to the idea, if it is sensible the likelihood is that they will be inclined to discuss it sensibly. Don't just think in terms of the technical aspects of the equipment itself, important as that is. Consider what is going into the equipment, e.g. metal panels to an automatic welding machine, or information to a minicomputer, and where the output will go.

Think about the people involved in feeding material or information into the machine, those operating the machine, those who will be drawing materials or information from the machine. Often changes which are consequent upon a machine being introduced, can easily be overlooked. A lot of jobs will change – including yours. A skilled turner may have to supervise several computer-controlled machines rather than operating one. One of your people may be operating a word processor cum computer, dealing with both the accounts and correspondence instead of just typing letters and doing the filing. You may be able to call up accounting data on the screen rather than delving through the books.

Figure 17 gives a checklist for introducing new equipment.

Knock-on effects

Some people think in terms of introducing technology to do one part of what they were doing before, and fondly imagine that little else will change. The fact is that if you want to get value for money out of the new equipment you will often need to review thoroughly just what you are doing and why. (See Figure 17.)

Example 1 You introduce a new device into the workshop which is faster than the old one and makes a better product. How will you adapt your storage space and the other parts of the process to keep pace with the new machine? Will you need buffer stocks to make sure there are always enough raw items ready for welding or milling, or goods ready for the microelectronically controlled painting machine?

Example 2 Many firms install a microcomputer but get only a fraction of the value from it because they fail to recognize how much better controlled information it can produce and how much more efficient their company could become if the power of the machine was used to the full. Often the training provided is sufficient to use the equipment routinely with the standard 'software' packages provided, but not enough to enable the small firm to tap the full potential of the microcomputer. It is worth spending a little time comparing one machine with another and checking up on back-up services and compatibility with other machines you may wish to add in later. Back-up here means technical advice, as well as spares and servicing arrangements. In the case of computers it also means software packages and the ability to link them to each other and to devices like printers of various kinds.

Involving your people As you think through what kind of machine you want, and how it will fit into your firm and its work and information flows, there are two very good reasons why you should involve your people in discussions. One reason is because it will lessen their fears by increasing their understanding of the issues involved and your reasons for wanting to make this move. Furthermore, through their experience of the job they will be able to make useful comments on the alternatives in terms of both equipment and working procedures. Don't forget the ergonomic factors – how people will sit or stand, whether they can reach and see everything they need to do without stretching and straining, whether the keyboard or the lathe has a firm, positive action. If your people have got to work at it for hours on end these things matter. If they are involved in the discussions, they are more likely to support the decisions with a measure of enthusiasm.

Training Once you decide to place the order, you must also decide on how to train your people – and perhaps yourself – so that you may get the machine working quickly and making its contribution to the business:

- Have you decided where to put it and arranged for power supplies and so forth?
- Have you decided who will operate the machine?
- No doubt you have thought about who will work it when the operator is away for any reason. Thus there will be at least two people who will need training.
- If you are making extra demands on these people, how do you propose to reward them?
- If you offer them an increased salary, how will this affect other workers?

Figure 17 *Introducing new equipment*

	Some key issues	Some people issues
First thoughts	What is the need for new equipment? What will it achieve for the firm? What changes will it make to working methods and to working relationships?	How will it affect the number of people employed? How is it likely to change people's jobs – and yours? How will you gain the commitment of your people to new procedures?
Collecting data	What alternatives are available and what are their relative merits and costs? How will they fit with other parts of your organization?	What demands will the alternatives make on your people? How will you benefit from the experience of your people as you make your choice?
Placing order	What are the running costs, maintenance arrangements and delivery times? What are the leasing or purchasing arrangements?	How will you prepare people for new skills and new roles?
Installation	Is the equipment safe, and working efficiently?	How – and when – will you see that people are trained (a) to work the equipment, (b) to operate new procedures and (c) to carry out routine maintenance?
Maintenance	Are the working conditions satisfactory – e.g. in terms of heating, lighting, space, noise, working positions, safety?	
Review	Is the equipment making its expected contribution to efficiency and effectiveness?	Are the people competent and content with the new equipment and arrangements?

Note These questions are indicative not exhaustive.

- Would it be worth retraining all the group (which might be say four or five people) and using them flexibly with a modest increase in salary?
- Have you included this in your financial estimate of the value of the new equipment and the time taken to recoup the outlay and show a net gain? (Incidentally if you are unionized you will need to renegotiate wage rates if you change the content of jobs.)
- If the new equipment you intend to introduce will mean that you will need fewer workers, how will you deal with that?
- Can you operate without making anyone redundant, e.g. by phasing the introduction with someone's retirement?

These things are not easy to organize in small firms but they are very real questions to consider.

Making people redundant If you feel you must make someone redundant, how will this be done? Last in first out? Or will you offer early retirement to someone with a golden hand-shake? Or is there one, very clearly defined job that will no longer need to be done? If you go for the unwelcome route of declaring one or two people redundant, then you must be sure you conform to the law's requirements. You have two major considerations from the business angle, and a major consideration on humanitarian grounds. Declaring someone redundant will cost money. No doubt you put that into your financial forecasts. Making someone redundant will also not do much for the confidence and morale of those who remain. They will wonder who will be next. Lastly, you may wish to be as generous and helpful as possible to the person (or people) concerned. It is common to give people more than the statutory minimum in terms of redundancy payments. You may help them to cope by directing them to sources of help and advice. You may do all you can to help them find alternative employment. This is not merely good human relations, it will help you to maintain sound working relationships with the people who remain.

Taking on more people On the other hand, you may wish to take on more people as your productive capacity is increased by technology. The new people may be needed either to work the new machines or, more likely, to ensure that the other functions in the enterprise keep pace. For example if your new equipment increases your production, you may need more sales people! Think carefully about the phasing of the recruitment and training of these new people. Remember that equipment costs money and the only way to make it pay is to use it to the full from the word go. That means making sure there is enough work for the machine, enough people to operate and maintain it and enough demand for its output. Don't forget that if capital investment is not matched by appropriate people investment, you are going to waste money. Recruitment and training are covered in later Units.

Getting going

Let's suppose that you have now trained your people, taken delivery of the machine and installed it. You will need to check on all the safety and working conditions points. These were covered in general terms in Unit 4. You will need to look at safety, not only in terms of the equipment itself, but also the changes it will bring about in the surrounding area e.g. the flow of work in the workshop, and perhaps storage of raw materials or partly finished goods, or the movement of people in an office.

You will need to observe work-flows and information flows very carefully and in particular look out for any unforeseen snags or unwanted side effects. At this stage the commitment and enthusiasm of your people is crucial.

Most equipment has what we call 'teething' troubles – those niggling little things that go wrong before you and your people have got accustomed to its idiosyncracies, and those adjustments which seem more critical than others in making it work properly. If your people are enthusiastic about the new tool and want to see it become a success, they will look upon each of these little problems as a challenge to be overcome, and will take a pride in mastering the machinery.

On the other hand, if you have not carried your people along with you, every one of those little problems will be regarded as proof-positive that you have made a serious mistake. They will point out all its defects and let you know, one way or another, that things were better before you brought in this new fangled device that is more trouble than it is worth. Managers undervalue the impact of these human traits and wonder why wonderful machines do not deliver the goods.

Reviewing

When these initial problems have been overcome you will want to review how the new machinery if doing, what contribution it is making to the firm, and whether your financial forecasts are going to hold up. Be sure to discuss these issues – as appropriate – with the people who are close to the problem. They will often tell you things which you may not be able to observe on the occasions when you drop in to see how it's going. If you share with key employees what you hope to get out of the equipment, they may well be able to make suggestions on how to develop its use, or how other parts of the process can be modified.

It is worth checking at the same time how people feel about using the equipment, how they find the working conditions, whether it is boring or more interesting. You may discover ways of enriching people's jobs and improving their morale and effectiveness. All in all, the more you can make the introduction and management of technology a joint adventure, the more return you will get on your investment.

Action Guidelines

1 If you are considering some new machinery or technological innovations in your firm, at what stage will you raise this with your people?

2 Will any of your people be involved in the choice of equipment?

3 How will you discuss with your people the changes in job content and any new wage structures or payment systems that will be required?

4 Which of your people will have need of new knowledge and skills? How will you arrange for the necessary training?

5 How will you check that the new equipment is being used properly and people are happy with it?

15
Leadership

- You can be a good leader, not by copying someone else, but by being yourself, by developing some insights and building your skills.

- Recognize what gives you satisfaction, how you see yourself, the way you tackle problems and take decisions.

- As you become sensitive to these things and the way you behave, you will be able to modify your behaviour to get better results.

- In this way you can work through your own personality to lead and help people to achieve improved performance.

Your management style

The whole image of the firm and its character are derived from the character and leadership qualities of its founder. This can last for generations. Your own style of management will have a profound impact on the firm. By now you will have realized that managing people is not a matter of obeying a set of simple rules in an automatic kind of way. Indeed one of the keys to success is to vary your response and way of dealing with people according to the particular situation at the time. Furthermore, just as the people we manage are all different, so all managers are different, and what may work well for one person and be easy to do may be difficult and perhaps disastrous for someone else.

The way to be a better manager, then, is not to try to copy some mythical 'ideal' manager, but to develop your own personality and behaviour, to become more aware of what you are doing in management terms and to be more in control of that aspect of your work. Some bosses seem to be very proud of managing 'by the seat of their pants' and give the impression that good management comes naturally. That may be true – for a very few people. Unfortunately there are a lot of people who are kidding themselves into believing they are good managers, when those around know that this is far from the truth. Furthermore, most of us who try to manage people need to strive constantly to be better, and to be sensitive to the changes taking place in society and the people who work for us.

Your motivation

In this Unit, therefore, we are going to focus for a while on you, the boss, the entrepreneur, the manager. How do you deal with people? How can you gain some insights into this problem? Let us have a look at Figure 18. Do not be alarmed by it. There is no need to complete it if you don't want to, but do take time to consider each of the issues raised. As in previous figures, this is not a scientific tool, just a way to help you think about what is important to you and how you are likely to react in different situations. There are no right or wrong answers, only responses that are more or less helpful in given situations.

Let us look at item 1. You might quite rightly say that you are concerned about all of these issues. But you are a strange person if all of them appeal to you in the same way. The scientist or engineer is more likely to be interested in science or engineering than in whether the firm does exciting things or makes quality products – although the other things matter. The entrepreneur will be more interested in seeing things happen and seizing opportunities than in being careful over the quality of the firm's goods or the fact that the team pulls together. The entrepreneur will need to ensure that the quality of goods is maintained, and that the team works well, otherwise the firm will not take off. The skilled craftsman will find satisfaction in seeing high quality goods being made. Do you begin to get the message? All aspects are important, but to many people one aspect is the driving force, and the others are means to that end.

Figure 18 *Managerial style*

Consider each of the ideas below. You might find it stimulating to try to allocate 10 marks between the items in each case, e.g. you might allocate 5 marks to 1*(a)*, 4 marks to 1*(b)*, 1 mark to 1*(c)* and zero to 1*(d)*. The answers are not, of course, mutually exclusive. You may well give a different answer in different circumstances.

1 My main concern in working in the business is:
   (a) to be really good at the trade or profession I am working at, e.g. electronic engineer, car salesman, jobbing printer
   (b) to make things really happen and to see the firm taking off and doing exciting things, to seize every opportunity to develop the business
   (c) to see that the goods produced by my firm or the services provided are really good quality and fully meet the demands of the market-place
   (d) to see that the people working for me are all pulling together to do something really worthwhile for the benefit of the company.

2 My primary aim as a manager is:
   (a) to see that my people really know where we are going and what we are aiming to achieve so that they can each play their part
   (b) to see that my people are treated fairly, rewarded when they do well and corrected constructively when they make mistakes
   (c) to gain the respect and support of my people and to know that they will work well without being constantly overlooked
   (d) to get my people working hard on the task in hand and doing what they are told
   (e) to ensure that my people do things correctly and according to the rules and procedures laid down
   (f) to ensure that the standards of work are maintained at a high level at all times.

3 My response to technical questions from my people is:
   (a) to give them an instant solution and to tell them what to do to put things right – without any need for explanations

Figure 18 – *continued*

   (b) to ask them further questions so that I can probe the problem and their understanding of it

   (c) to give them a quick interpretation of the situation as I see it, on the basis of what they say

   (d) to encourage them to pursue their own line of thinking and to see where it leads.

4 My attitude to taking decisions is:

   (a) to take them myself and to tell people what I have decided

   (b) to take decisions and then to convince my people that the decisions are fully justified

   (c) to talk about matters with my people and then to make decisions myself, taking their views into account

   (d) to talk about matters with my people and to try to reach agreement on how to proceed

   (e) to delegate decisions to my people as much as I can

Flexibility

What has this got to do with managing people? A great deal. What motivates you to run the business also influences your attitude to people and the way you relate to them. It is very likely to endow you with a particular way of working. That is not wrong – unless it is the only way you can operate. As we have seen before, the secret of success in managing people is to be flexible enough to change the way you do it if the circumstances change. You may have noticed that in the preceding paragraph no example was given for 1(d), the person who gets his satisfaction from getting people working well together. I suppose that generally speaking people like that do not run small firms, but get into public service or community work. Nevertheless, if that is what you enjoy, there's no reason why you should not make a successful businessman provided you have due regard to the other issues – providing goods or services for the market (or markets) at the right price, quality and time.

Self-image

Let us move on to the second question, which looks at how you see yourself in relation to your people. Notice that your answers will portray your self-image. That may not be (indeed probably will not be) how others see you. It is a difficult thing to see ourselves as others do, and it is outside the scope of this book to describe how this problem can be approached. You can improve your self-image (making it more accurate, not more flattering!) by thinking over some concrete experiences soon after they have occurred. You may be in for a surprise. You may find you are not as tough and single-minded as you thought – or as benevolent! Since the exercise is for your own good, and for the benefit of the firm, be as ruthlessly honest with yourself as you can. Most of us fail to live up to our self-image, but as we become aware of this failing we have an opportunity to put it right.

Scientists and engineers The scientist or engineer-type will probably favour 2*(c)*, because such people tend to attach a lot of importance to people being individually responsible and competent at their jobs. Such managers do not want to look over the shoulders of their people, because they want to spend time on their first love, the science, technology or aspect of engineering which brought them into the business in the first place. If you fall into this group to any extent (and none of the groups have hard and fast limits), you may find you have to put a bit of extra effort into making some people follow through and do what you expect of them at a reasonable cost and in a reasonable time. You may find quality controls and so forth irksome, but they are necessary. Everyone is not as keen as you are on your special subject.

Entrepreneurs The entrepreneur-type might favour 2*(a)*, because it is the direction of the firm – the new initiatives, the leading edge – which matters. The entrepreneur will have little patience with rules and regulations, and may have a tendency to be a bit intolerant of people who make mistakes. There is no time to be wasted gaining people's respect, after all trading is the name of the game. People must work well when they see how exciting it all is. Once more if you are somewhat like this, you have the makings of a fine leader – but you must not ride rough-shod over people's feelings and expect them to serve you loyally into the bargain. You may need to force yourself to give a little time to these concerns. You must also see that certain rules are obeyed – especially in the health and safety field, and that your paperwork is in order for the authorities, as well as for your own purposes.

Craftsmen The craftsman-type person may favour 2(f), since high quality workmanship is the prime motivator. That is fine, and many people will work happily for such a person recognizing legitimate concern to produce something really worthwhile. Many people will respond well to this situation. But if you are like this, do be particularly careful to be constructive in your criticisms as you strive for quality, and to recognize the important work of people who perform tasks in your firm other than the production of goods. Do not behave as if the clerk or the salespeople are somehow second-class, because they do not have your skills.

Technical questions

We have looked at question 3 a little in the Unit on talking and listening to people, but at this point we are considering the matter in a different context – your personal style and preferences. The scientist/engineer type will tend to be a prober, more interested in the question than in its solution. The entrepreneur will be more interested in a quick resolution of the problem – and to provide it – than concerned with explanations or excuses. The craftsman-type will be interested in the technical issues at stake and how a high quality, lasting solution can be found. Interpretation of the problem may be a key issue. Few managers in small firms will encourage people to develop their own ideas about products and services. The exception may be in firms where creativity is at a high premium, e.g. an advertising agency.

There is no ideal general response, but if you have a pronounced tendency to always respond in the same way, you should try to develop a kind of mental check on your behaviour. This will enable you to widen the scope of your responses, to increase your repertoire, as it were.

The next step is to try to get better at matching the response to the needs of the situation and the person who brings along the problem.

Decision-making

We have to some extent discussed decision-making in Unit 5. Typically the scientist-engineer type will want to delegate decisions to other people so that more time can be given to technical matters, whereas the entrepreneur will want to take all the decisions personally and fast – so there will be no time for discussions and debates. The craftsman will want to be sure the decision is right, and may for that reason want to talk things over with the people. It is probably true to say that for many managers in small firms there is not much inclination to spend time talking about decisions. Decisions are there to be taken, not savoured like a tasty morsel of food. But as we have seen before, the effective manager will recognize when it is wise to enter into discussions with the top team and/or with the workforce, because they are vitally involved and their commitment is essential to success in the enterprise.

Action Guidelines

1 Do you have a clearer picture of your own management style – having studied Figure 18?

2 Are there aspects of your management style which need to be developed?

3 What will you do to develop specific aspects of your management style to improve your effectiveness?

4 How can you develop flexibility in the way you manage?

5 What management styles do you wish to emphasize in your senior staff? How will you encourage this?

16
Hiring More People

- First you must decide what the newcomer will be expected to do. You must try to envisage what kind of skills the person will need.
- Then you will need to attract applicants, and deal with the people who apply.
- There's no foolproof method of selection, but you can increase the odds in your favour.
- You will want to interview, but beware of the pitfalls, and see if there are other ways in which you can assess people's ability to do the job.

Another person

For a small firm, taking on another person is a big step. It means that the firm – with the extra person – must earn enough money to pay the extra salary and meet the other employment costs. The newcomer will also need space to work in and equipment to use, whether it is another delivery van, a lathe or a table and chair. But in many ways the most important, yet the most difficult problem, is to find someone who will not only do the job well, but also fit harmoniously into the existing team. If you are unfortunate enough to hire someone who causes discord among your people, you have a very difficult time ahead.

Selecting the right person is not easy, and there is no foolproof way of doing it. There are a number of ways, however, in which you can improve the odds on getting someone who is satisfactory. The more sophisticated methods of selection are probably beyond the means of small firms – they take a lot of time and cost a lot of money. Nevertheless, there are some fairly simple steps you can take. Most jobs are filled by word of mouth, by advertising in the local paper, or by contact with the local Jobcentre or employment exchange. Whatever method you use, you should begin by thinking rather carefully about what job you want done and the skills required to do it. We shall discuss later how you recruit specialists or graduates.

In Unit 2 we discussed how to get out a simple 'job description' for the people who already work for you. If you are simply trying to replace one of these people because they are leaving or being moved to a different (perhaps better) job, then you can use the existing job description as a starting point:

- Is it up to date?
- Does it cover the really important points?

You will find it useful to discuss the document with the jobholder before he leaves or moves on. This time probe more deeply those areas where attitudes, knowledge or skills seem to be most crucial for success.

On the other hand you may want to add someone extra to take part of the load off some of your people (maybe you too!) or to do some new task which has not been done before, or done only at a much lower level, or sub-contracted out. Whether the new person is a replacement or doing a new job, the opportunity should not be missed to review the current range of duties of your key people. Adding another member to the team may enable you to redistribute duties and responsibilities in better ways in the light of your experience. You may be able to redistribute workloads, or to reallocate responsibilities in ways which line up better with people's strengths and weaknesses. You may be able to enrich somebody's job because you think the person has more potential. If you consider these things before you finally decide what sort of extra person you want, you can then try to recruit and select accordingly.

Writing down the job

Having decided what job you want done, you must now try to get a few notes down in writing. You may find it useful to use the 'Recruitment job description' form in Figure 19. You will notice that this is different to the one in Figure 3, because it has a different purpose. The description in Figure 3 was to help discuss the job with the jobholder. The form in Figure 11 is to help you to recruit the right person to fill the job. Since you do not have a jobholder, there's no space for a name. There is an extra space, however, for you to try to summarize – perhaps in a sentence of about twenty words – what the job is about. This will be most useful if you want to discuss it with someone in a Jobcentre or Employment Agency, or to compose an advertisement in a newspaper, or to put on a postcard in the local shop window or to put on a noticeboard outside the works.

The next two headings are straightforward. The tabular part is most important and will require some effort on your part, but do not shirk it.

Try to think about the new job in two or three different ways:

- You might, for example, ask yourself what 'outputs' you expect from the person, i.e. what are the achievements of the job.
- If you want to recruit a shorthand typist, what dictation speed do you want, and what typing speed?
- What will the ancillary duties be, e.g. petty cash, answering simple letters, answering the telephone, simple filing?
- If you want to recruit a book-keeper, will the person be required to deal with customers, e.g. chasing bad debts, to fill out and distribute wage packets (and deal with queries), to be responsible for following up purchase orders – as well as to keep the accounts in order and to deal with the Inland Revenue, Customs and Excise and your firm's accountant?
- If you want a borer, do you require him or her to do vertical as well as horizontal boring?

Figure 19 *Recruitment job description*

JOB TITLE:

ONE SENTENCE SUMMARY:

JOBHOLDER REPORTS TO:

PEOPLE REPORTING TO JOBHOLDER (IF ANY):

MAIN RESPONSIBILITIES	ATTRIBUTES NEEDED
(list, with a brief note on each one)	
KEY CONTACTS	
(list, with a brief note on each one)	

Do be as specific as you can. Then we move on to the list of key contacts. Are some of these contacts particularly demanding, e.g. relations with customers, overseas clients who do not speak English, technical people? Alongside each entry in the responsibilities and key contact columns, see if you can write down any quality you are looking for in the newcomer. Do not set your standards higher than you need to in any particular case. It is not unknown for managers to want people to take dictation faster than they can dictate. Sheer typing speed is rarely the most important factor when choosing a secretary or a shorthand typist. Accuracy counts, especially, for example, in a medical or legal practice. If the person concerned will be expected to answer simple letters, specify the ability to do just that in the right-hand column. Answering the telephone means being able to listen and also to talk clearly and distinctly. Be careful to specify precisely any technical requirements in the job, whether at the craft or technician level, or in the clerical and commercial sphere.

- Will any ability with figures be required?
- For the book-keeper, will the ability to use a minicomputer be required?
- When you start to think about the people the newcomer will deal with – especially outside the firm – what qualities will you look for in an applicant?
- Is the contact only by mail, or by telephone or face to face?
- If contacts are face to face or by telephone, then again the ability to listen and to speak clearly and distinctly are obvious requirements.

But there is more. In dealing with clients one needs to be polite, tactful and persuasive. If that's true in your business, write it down. If you're dealing with poor payers you may need to be politely firm, or even tough and resilient. Will the person need to stand up to abuse from irate callers? You may need to specify even temper! Will the person need to talk with technical people? Perhaps customers who want a special job done will want to talk about their needs in some detail. This may be a task for your craftsman, not your secretary. If you have a lot of dealings with a foreign country you may need to recruit someone who speaks, reads and writes in a foreign language. Do be careful to specify the ability to converse as well as to correspond in writing.

Building up the person you want

By now you should be assembling a formidable list of qualities you require. You can begin to build up a simple pen-portrait, in note form, of the kind of person you want to recruit – see Figure 20.

Why not show this to some of the people in your firm who will need to work with the newcomer? They may have some helpful suggestions or improvements. Do realize that the time you spend now could save you hundreds of hours later, because if you make the wrong choice you will have a great deal of extra work both while that person works for you and when you come to replace him or her.

But do not expect to get just what you want. Look for people who have the ability to do the job, or for people who have the ability to learn how to do it. Be careful not to exclude people on grounds that are irrelevant, e.g. race, sex or age. (Do not forget the legislation on race relations and equal pay.) If you feel you want an experienced person, say so, but it is rarely wise to limit the field by age. If you have a salary bracket in mind, you can say this as well.

It may sound strange, but do not always go for what seems to be the most able applicant. Someone who is too good for the job is

Figure 20 *Recruitment and selection*

1 Decide on what job you want the newcomer to do. Write it down.

2 Decide on the kind of person you need to do the job, in terms of abilities – knowledge and skill – and also in terms of attitudes and the ability to fit into your existing team of people.

3 Decide on what further steps you will take to find the right person.

4 Make the job known.

5 Screen applicants.

6 Select, by means of interview.

7 Make an offer.

unlikely to be happy in it for long unless there are some special circumstances. Be especially careful not to over-emphasize academic ability. There is plenty of evidence for the fact that people without formal academic qualifications can be creative and capable of doing demanding jobs, sometimes involving disciplined mental as well as manual skills.

Ways of recruiting

Let's suppose you have simple notes about the job and about the kind of person you want to recruit. How do you let people know? That depends on the job. If you want someone to deliver newspapers to the local estate, a postcard in the shop window, or simply to spread the word amongst your existing staff may do the trick. If you want an engineering craftsman or a cook, an advertisement in the local newspaper and a chat with your local Jobcentre may prove successful. If you want a lot of engineering craftsmen it may be better to advertise in a local paper in the Midlands or the North East where there are a number of unemployed but highly skilled people. You must, however, consider whether people moving into your area can find accommodation. Don't forget the Careers Service if you are looking for a youngster. If you want to recruit a graduate or a specialist, e.g. personnel manager, accountant or biochemist or someone with unique experience or abilities, e.g. a knowledge of the Arab world, or of exporting to North America, you will have to consider more carefully how you go about it. What sort of organizations do they belong to, what magazines and newspapers do they read, who keeps lists of people in that category looking for jobs? We shall return to the question of specialists and graduates later, but the basic idea is to look at this from the potential applicant's end.

If you want to recruit someone very special – say someone who will ultimately run the whole business while you take a back seat and ease into retirement – you will want to be very careful indeed. This is something you should try to anticipate three or four years ahead of your intended date of retirement. Some firms specialize in recruiting managers, and some – the so-called 'headhunters' will help you draw up a specification and then go out and find such a person. This is expensive, but often worth the money to a large company. Its value is more doubtful for a small company, because these executive search firms tend to work mainly with the larger enterprises.

Getting down to details Having chosen how to make the vacancy known, you must consider exactly what you will say in the notice or advertisement, or what information you will give to the Employment Agency or Jobcentre. You will wish to consider carefully the cost of advertisements and the charges required by Employment Agencies. The details should include the title of the job (which must make it clear that the post can be filled by a man or woman), a simple description of the duties, hours of work, location of the job and where further details can be obtained. It is generally better to specify a salary range or a minimum wage rate. The exception is when you want to be free to negotiate an employee remuneration package which depends on the kind of person who applies. Even here it is usually worth quoting a minimum figure.

One of the things you must judge is how many applicants you are likely to get, and whether you want to increase or decrease the number. It's a terrible chore wading through hundreds of application forms. On the other hand it is disheartening (and expensive) to get a very low response, especially if the quality of the applicants is inappropriate. You can increase the number by emphasizing any special features you are offering – like 'car provided', 'generous fringe benefits' or 'profit-sharing scheme'. Be careful to match the kind of benefit with the potential applicant. It's no good emphasizing the beautiful location of your headquarters if you are recruiting a salesman who will be 'on the road' most of the time. He wants to hear that you offer a competitive basic wage and generous commission on sales! The research scientist will be attracted by the thought of a 'well-equipped' laboratory. Choose the bait carefully.

If you want to cut down the number of applicants, specify the qualities required more closely – but be careful not to eliminate good quality applicants. You might say, for example, 'five years' experience in heavy goods vehicle maintenance work required', 'people earning less than £15,000 need not apply', 'honours degree in mechanical engineering or similar qualification necessary', 'good knowledge of computer programming essential'.

Dealing with applications

When people respond to your advertisement, perhaps with a letter or telephone call, you must react. If you have only a few applicants you might simply ask them to call in to see you, by appointment, but at some stage you will want some information from them, in writing. How much information depends on the job. This kind of information can be easily requested on an application form like the one in Figure 21, but don't ask for more information than you really need, especially if the job does not require a lot of academic qualifications. If you have a lot of people applying, you may ask them all to fill up a form and post it to you. You can then look through the forms and decide who to see. It may be necessary to limit the number of people you see – after all your time is money. Selecting people to see on the basis of forms is not very good, but you can make a better job of it if you decide beforehand the basis of your choice. Do you want people with certain qualifications, e.g. an engineering craftsman who has served an apprenticeship and obtained a City and Guilds certificate, HND or equivalent in Dental Technology, a typing speed of 60 words per minute, a book-keeper with a Grade II certificate of the Royal Society of Arts?

Interviewing

Let us suppose you have, by one means or another, decided to see five people and you want to select one for the job. The commonest method is the 'interview'. It's a pretty poor method of selection for most jobs and very often very badly carried out. There are two things you should do:

- First of all make sure you give each person a good, fair interview.
- Secondly, see if you can devise a way of finding out how the person might fare in action.

For example, get the shorthand typist to take down a brief letter and type it for you. Ask a draftsman to do a drawing. Get out an example of the book-keeping records and discuss it with the would-be book-keeper. Take the craftsman to the machine and chat with him

Figure 21 *Application form*

NAME (block capitals, surname first):

DATE OF BIRTH:

ADDRESS:

TELEPHONE NUMBER (if any):

Name and address of present or previous employer (no contact will be made with this employer without your express permission):

Signature _____   Date _____

Note You can add more questions if you are sure they are relevant, for example:

EDUCATIONAL QUALIFICATIONS (please give subjects, dates, examination bodies concerned and grades or honours levels attained):

EMPLOYMENT EXPERIENCE (please give job title, dates, employer and final salary in each case):

OTHER QUALIFICATIONS OR RELEVANT EXPERIENCE:

OTHER INTERESTS, HOBBIES ETC. (Note: this is generally speaking of very little value in selection):

Note This form and the language should be kept as short and simple as possible.

about how he would tackle a certain kind of job. The nearer you can get to the real job, the more likely you are to learn whether the person would be successful.

A quiet place You must make a serious attempt to find a quiet place for the interviews and to see that you are not disturbed. You can't expect to have a sensible conversation with someone on such an important matter if the telephone keeps ringing and people keep dashing in and out. When people come to an interview which matters to them, they are generally a bit nervous and not their ordinary selves. If you want to get closer to the real person, do what you can to reduce that tension. A quiet room helps. Try not to bear down on them from across a cluttered desk. Start the conversation on something which they will find easy to talk about, like where they live and how easy, or difficult, it was to get to the interview. Don't make this part seem like an inquisition. Make congenial conversation for a minute or two. Not for too long, but a couple of minutes helping the individual to settle down will produce a more fruitful interview.

Beware of first impressions, and do not judge by appearances. Contrary to popular opinion, you can now tell very little about people's ability to do jobs from the cut of their clothes or hair, or the colour of their socks and jeans. Try to overcome the temptation to judge people on the quality of their speech or pronunciation – unless of course it is an essential (and I mean ESSENTIAL) qualification for the job.

Structuring the interview You will need to move quickly into the structured part of the interview, based on the qualities you are looking for. Break them down into say five groups or items. Make sure you cover each group in each interview, and after each interview (NOT during it) write a few words against each item for the candidate you have just seen. After the interviews you should have five comments on each candidate, which will help you to remember them and to make a reasoned – hopefully unbiased – decision as to whether one of them can really do the job and fit into your team. Keep these notes as they will come in handy should someone later say that you chose the person unfairly. Make sure your choice is based on suitability for the job and is not clouded by irrelevant matters like sex, colour or racial origin.

You will need to take special care to ensure that you do not – even subconsciously – reject someone who is otherwise suitable, on grounds of race or sex.

Before you end the interview, be sure you have given the applicant an opportunity to ask you questions about the job and the working conditions, salary and so forth, and that you have made it clear what action you propose to take, e.g. please wait outside for a few minutes, or I'll be writing to tell you my decision in a week or two. Then be sure you do what you have said. It is very bad form to leave people in the dark for weeks. If you can't decide for a month or whatever, make this plain to the people concerned.

Job offer

When you have made your choice you must write or speak to the individual concerned. At some stage you must write down the precise terms and conditions you are offering, and ask for a written reply within a reasonable period. As soon as you have filled the post, it is a matter of courtesy to inform the unsuccessful applicants. Make it clear to the newcomer when he or she should come and to whom they should report. We shall take up the story of what follows in Unit 19.

We have assumed throughout this Unit that you will recruit people personally. If you delegate this to someone, make sure they know how to do the job properly and make it clear to them exactly what discretion they may exercise.

Action Guidelines

1 Having decided what job has to be filled and what sort of person you are seeking, what are the various methods of getting applicants?

2 How do you select people for interview?

3 How do you prepare for these interviews? What questions do you ask and what information do you give?

4 Consider what tests or other methods you can use to improve your selection. Can you choose some everyday tasks performed in your firm and adapt them into short tests?

5 What is your policy on employing coloured people? Have you a clear policy on employing women? How can you avoid unfair discrimination?

17
Hiring a Specialist

- Consider first just why you need a specialist. It is important to make sure the person has the sort of expertise you need.
- It is critical to ensure that the person can fulfil the role you have in mind and fit into your existing workforce.
- There are, in many cases, specialist journals you can advertise in. You are likely to need expert assistance in the selection process unless you are an expert in the specialist area yourself.
- Do not expect a specialist to passively accept the duties you prescribe. If the person recruited is any good at all, he or she will want to discuss the duties with you and to agree on the best way they can contribute to the firm.

The need for a specialist

In Unit 16 we considered the recruitment of people in general, but you may need to recruit someone rather special to work in your firm. This may arise because of specialization, diversification or expansion.

Specialization Your business may be specialist in nature, e.g. if you are manufacturing foodstuffs, processing chemicals, or producing sophisticated electronic devices. You may be offering professional services in the field of accountancy, marketing or management development. In such cases you are probably well aware of the kind of people you might recruit, the organizations they belong to and the qualifications they could be expected to possess.

Diversification Another reason for recruiting a specialist might be connected with diversification. If, for example, your business is such that you have regular large influxes of cash, you might want to set up a small venture to use that cash, and you therefore have a need for someone with expertise in using cash. Or you might have bought a computer or word processor and found that you have a lot of spare capacity which could be used as the basis of another business which might run alongside your main operation. But you do not want the distraction of running this yourself, and so want to hire someone to run it for you.

Expansion A third reason for recruiting a specialist arises when your firm expands to the point where you want to delegate more responsibility, perhaps in an aspect of business that does not interest you. For example, you might be a scientist who has set up a successful small firm and now wants a businessman to take over a lot of the marketing and sales side of things. On the other hand you might be an entrepreneur who is more interested in marketing your products and you want a good production engineer to run the factory for you, or an accountant to deal with all the 'in-house' financial and administrative chores. It is really important to think through why you need the specialist and what role you look to him or her to carry out:

- Do you want a first-class boffin who will be tucked away in the background producing really first-class ideas which can be the basis of new products or services?
- Or do you want a person to ensure your production is really cost-effective, your quality high and your specification and labelling in full conformity to the law, e.g. in the case of food, drugs, children's toys and so forth.

Criteria for selection

In selecting a specialist to work in your firm you have three prime considerations:

- The person's technical knowledge and competence in the field that matters to you.

- The individual's personal qualities in relation to the role you have in mind.
- The way he or she will fit into the ongoing work of the firm.

Let us take each of these items in turn.

Technical knowledge First of all, do not assume that because a person has a degree in chemistry, for example, that that guarantees expertise at a high level in the kind of chemistry that matters in your firm. This may be highly specialized. Indeed you may find it very difficult to find a real expert if you work in certain fields. There are a lot of food chemists and petrochemists around, but not so many experts in wax chemistry. If you are a specialist in this area yourself, you will want to probe the particular field of interest at the interview stage. If you are not a specialist, you would be wise to call in someone who is to help you draw up the person-specification, and to take part in the interview with you. In this way you will be able to select a candidate who is most likely to quickly acquire the particular knowledge and skills you require. (You might need to accelerate this process by sending the individual on a course or to spend some time at a university to get this expertise.)

Real experts are expensive and this emphasizes the need for sound selection and for getting maximum value for money quickly. If you do not know any experts you can turn to for help in this selection process, where can you go?

There are three alternatives you might consider:

- One is to visit the appropriate department of a local university or polytechnic. In some cases there are people there with a practical bent who will be prepared to spend a little time helping you.
- Another possibility is to turn to the appropriate professional body, e.g. for scientists, bodies like the Royal Society of Chemistry, the Institute of Biology; for architects or surveyors, bodies like the Royal Institute of British Architects, the Royal Institution of Chartered Surveyors; for engineers, bodies like the Institution of Mechanical Engineers, the Institution of Electronic and Radio Engineers; for experts in sales and

marketing, bodies like the Institute of Marketing; for personnel and training people, bodies like the Institute of Personnel Management or the Institute of Training and Development. The list is enormous. There are over a dozen different kinds of engineering institution, and about half a dozen different accountancy bodies. You can find a reasonably up-to-date list in the latest *Whitaker's Almanack*. Since these bodies regard themselves as having a responsibility not only to their members, but also to the proper conduct of the profession, they will mostly want to help you get a suitable person. Some of these bodies keep lists of their members who are looking for new jobs.

- If what you want is someone who is a specialist in a particular sector of industry, you might find it useful to approach the relevant trade association or employer's association, e.g. the Food Manufacturers' Federation, the British Cement Manufacturers' Federation, the Jute Spinners and Manufacturers' Association, the Federation of Small Mines of Great Britain, the Engineering Employers' Federation, or the National Federation of Building Trades Employers. Since these bodies exist to serve their members interests, you can expect much more help if you are a member. Again a list is to be found in *Whitakers Almanack*.

Personal qualities The second issue is the role, particularly in terms of interpersonal relationships, that you hope your specialist will fill. Unfortunately the university courses for scientists and engineers often fail to pay adequate attention to the human relations side of science and engineering based industries. We shall return to the subject of graduates fresh from college in the next Unit, but here it is necessary to stress the point that scientists and engineers – especially some of the younger ones – are not too good at dealing with people. But there are many who can deal effectively with people. **The key question is, how important is it to you?**

You may be fortunate enough to find someone with a first-class honours degree, and possibly with a higher degree as well, who is very good at gaining the co-operation of others. Make that person an offer quick (provided that other things are equally good). On the other hand you may find you have to choose, in the end, between a very highly competent expert who does not relate well to other people, or a reasonably good, but not brilliant, person who does. If you want your firm to be at the leading edge of the technology, you will choose the first person and make up your mind to manage this situation. If you are content to build slowly on your existing range of products, or to move forward more carefully from the existing technology in a new venture, then the second person may be the better choice. There is no simple answer but you must think through the issues before you advertise the post.

Recruitment

You are now ready to follow the procedure outlined in Unit 16. Here, however, you will want a lot of detail about the technical knowledge and skills required, and the kind of qualification and experience you will be seeking. These sections of both the job description and the person specification will need to be completed fully and carefully, perhaps with the help indicated above. This will also be reflected in the form which you ask applicants to complete. Professional people are used to filling in forms so it can be a bit longer for them. But don't ask questions that are irrelevant. That makes more work for them, and for you as well. Your next task is to get some applicants. You might try the 'old boy' network, or contact the professional bodies mentioned above. You might decide to advertise – in which case you want to select the magazine with great care. It is expensive to advertise and you want to make sure you use precisely those magazines which the specialist will read.

Advertising in journals Many of the professional bodies publish journals carrying job advertisements. There are also other commercial magazines which appeal to particular groups of specialists. Before you place an advertisement, thumb through a selection of the magazines, see what kinds of job are advertised, check on the number of magazines sold each month and so forth. If your vacancy is very different from all the others in the magazine it's clearly not worth putting it in. It is not generally a good idea to advertise this kind of job in a local paper unless you know that there are likely to be a lot of people with these qualifications in your area. It is not the place where most professional people look for jobs. The national newspapers are probably too expensive for a small firm, and you might find yourself swamped with replies that waste your time.

What to say in advertisements   What will you put in the advertisement? Clearly, the name and address of your firm, the job-title and generally a brief description of the job itself and an outline of the terms you are offering. If you want a particular qualification it is useful to indicate that, but it is rarely a good idea to be too exclusive. Use a phrase like 'candidates with a good honours degree in polymer chemistry will be preferred' or 'a degree in electrical engineering or an equivalent qualification required'. This signals to the reader that they must either have the qualification in question, or be able to offer something very similar which you might find acceptable. It is questionable what you should say about the salary offered. You must find out the going rate for the kind of job you have in mind and presumably you are prepared to pay it. Stating a salary bracket often helps people to make a judgement about the level of the job in relation to their current position and it should cut down on the number of grossly over- or under-qualified applicants. The problem is that it might put off a really good applicant to whom you would be prepared to offer a higher salary. Broadening the salary band you specify will encourage everyone who applies to push you to the upper end of the bracket. Another ploy is to set the bottom limit only, i.e. 'the salary payable will be at least £10,000 per annum . . .'.

If you advertise in more than one place it may be useful to code the replies in some way. For example, if you have a little cut-out reply slip to enable those interested to request an application form and further details, you can put the initials of the magazine in the corner. If you don't give a slip but ask people to write to you, you might say 'quoting reference PM2 in your reply' (for *Personnel Management*, February) or you might say 'reply to Dept PM2, Ash Machine Tool Company etc.'. This will help you, if you have to advertise again, to decide which advertisement medium gave you the most promising applicants.

Selection

Let's assume you now have some letters from people asking for more details. You can now send them an application form and more information – perhaps a duplicated sheet giving a more complete picture of your company, the vacancy and the qualities you seek in the applicants. Be careful here (as in the advertisement) to avoid any bias in terms of colour, race or sex. On seeing the details, some people may not move on to the next stage and send in a completed form. That's life. Be sure to give a closing date – a reasonable one. Allow for postal delivery times and give people a week or two to fill up the forms. If they are serious about the job they will want to think about what they put on the form, and in the covering letter. They will wish to slant the way they present their qualifications and experience to show you how it meets your needs. This is in no way dishonest and indeed it shows genuine interest. (I am assuming that no facts are falsified or material information withheld. You may need to put a declaration to this effect to be signed by the applicant at the end of the form.)

Drawing up a list of criteria The next step is to look through the completed forms and read the letters. Before you start, draw up a list of the four or five things you are especially looking for in the person. Then draw up a table and award some simple mark or a tick if the person has it. This is hardly necessary if you have only a few forms to look at, but even then it can be useful. It will not take long. You have then to decide whether to see everyone, or just a selection of the applicants. If you decide to select a few, you should be careful about the criteria you use. Throughout this whole process it is useful to involve a colleague or an expert, and this is particularly true at this sifting stage and in the interview. If this is not your area of expertise you may find it difficult to make judgements about the value of someone's experience in this job or that in the particular firms mentioned.

Interviewing the specialist Next, the interviews. You must decide whether to take up references before or after the interviews. You should not take up any references unless the applicant has explicitly given you permission to do so. If people are already in employment, then they will not generally want their employers to know that they are applying for other jobs. You must respect that confidence. If you take up references before the interview this might help you make a better choice. If you leave it until afterwards, you may need to write only to the referees of one person rather than six or seven. How will you invite people? It is not a good idea to spread the interviews over too long a period, or your memory of the first one will begin to fade before you have finished. Try to arrange them all within say one week. You may decide to set aside a whole day for the job. The interview must be long enough for you to make a judgement. In the case of specialists it is sometimes worth having a second interview with the most promising candidate (or perhaps two of them) before making a final decision. The second interview could be on another day. Interviews of this kind generally last from 30 to 45 minutes and may be longer. The general comments in Unit 16 apply here. Begin by some gentle, easy, non-threatening conversation, then move into three or four carefully selected technical areas, one at a time. If the candidate is clearly missing the point or ignorant of a specific area, move on to another area. You are trying to find out what the candidate knows and is capable of doing, not to embarrass him or her. A good way into the interview is to ask a few questions about previous jobs.

A most important question to ask is what the person thinks about the job being applied for in this particular case. Someone who can't talk about that in a sensible way is probably not a serious candidate. It is reasonable to expect a candidate to have formed some view about the job in prospect, even if that view is wrong in several respects. This issue should be raised near the end of the interview and can lead on to a brief – very brief – explanation by you about the job so that you can gauge the applicant's response to that. Finally you should allow the candidate to ask you a question or two and then make it clear what you intend to do next.

Job offer

Having selected the person you want you must then make an offer. In dealing wth people of this kind you may ultimately have to bargain a little. You can, however, get a very good idea of what remuneration package to offer by starting with the existing salary of the person concerned and any increases likely in the near future.

You will need to meet that figure and more. Secondly, if the individual needs to move house, especially if it means moving to a more expensive part of the country, they may need a higher salary to meet these expenses, and you should be able to estimate this. After adding a little more, at your discretion, as an incentive, this enables you to arrive at the figure you will aim at. It is a matter of judgement whether you offer this outright, or whether you hold back a little for bargaining purposes. The applicant will not take less than you offer, and may try to get more. You can always offer to increase the salary after three or six months subject to satisfactory performance – if you are sure you can measure this unequivocally. If not, you had better avoid this, as it could cause you a lot of arguments later.

This oral offer will need to be followed up by a written offer and at some stage you will want to take up references. This can be done between the oral and the written offer (if the candidate agrees) or you could make a written offer 'subject to satisfactory references'. If you do this, you imply that only if something damaging emerges from the referees which should have been revealed at interview will you go back on the offer. Legally, no doubt, you could withdraw the offer if you had other sufficient grounds based on new information, but if your interview was thorough and the application form sound you should not be in for any shocks from referees. **But it can happen**, and you should not omit this precaution.

Discussing the job description

When the specialist actually comes to work for you, there will be the job description to discuss. It is unwise to simply hand it over and expect the newcomer to work to it. Use it, rather, as a basis for discussion and for forging a new, mutually agreed, description of the job. Try to focus on outputs – what the jobholder achieves – rather than inputs, i.e. the tasks to be performed. See if you can work out some preliminary targets (as in Unit 6). If the specialist is any good the job will gradually change over time, hopefully becoming more productive, more positive and – for the jobholder – more challenging. In many jobs the tasks are initially assigned by management and these are subsequently modified by management. But specialists don't work that way. They use the initial job description as the starting point to create new roles which are often constantly changing and expanding.

Don't fight this development, become involved in it, and see that it works for the good of the firm. Some of the changes will be gradual, others incremental. The incremental steps may involve changes in the roles of other people to be fully effective. You can act as an intermediary and by managing these changes in roles and relationships you can shape the way your firm develops.

Action Guidelines

1 Before you advertise for a specialist in a discipline in which you are not an expert, how do you decide what type of person you want?

2 What help do you enlist to help you with your recruitment procedure?

3 How do you deal with the technical aspects of an applicant's previous experience and present knowledge during an interview?

4 What action do you take to explain to the specialist you have appointed, the limits of the new job and how you intend to monitor the individual's progress and performance?

18
Hiring a Graduate

- You may want a graduate in a specific subject, in which case you should read this Unit in conjunction with the preceding one.

- If, however, you want someone who is intelligent and keen, and able to contribute to your business, perhaps to question some of the things you do, there's a lot to be said for employing a young graduate.

- Graduates are not all alike. Many will not easily fit into a small firm, so you must do your best to get the right person.

- A graduate who wants a challenge and a change, and is prepared to muck in, will probably do very well, and there are many like that about.

Why a graduate?

Many proprietors of small firms seem to be reluctant to employ graduates and thus cut themselves off from a very valuable source of recruitment. The fact of the matter is that the overwhelming majority of academically able people remain in further or higher education and get degrees. There are exceptions, but they are few and far between. There are, of course, abilities other than the academic kind, and these are often equally valuable – but different. If you want people with brains, think about employing a graduate at some suitable point.

Some graduates take degrees that are clearly linked to an occupation or career – in law, accountancy, chemical engineering, medicine, estate management and so forth. Not all of them, however, find that they want to continue in that field when they graduate. There are a large number of graduates who study a variety of subjects which interest them, but who do not have any particular career bias. You therefore have a choice between hiring a graduate with an education and training which meets a specific need in your firm, e.g. for a mechanical engineer, a polymer technologist or a cost accountant, or hiring a graduate who is clearly intelligent, who will fit into your team and who is keen to learn the business.

Just as there is a reluctance to employ graduates, there is also a hesitation on the part of graduates when they consider working for a small firm. Why is this?

- They have got used to the idea of working in large organizations. (A university with less than 2,500 staff and students is small.)
- They see in large organizations a kind of career ladder which reaches to the top. (They often fail to calculate the odds of getting very far up it!)
- They see in a large firm the chance of moving to a fresh job every few years (hopefully with promotion!) and hence the chance of a varied career without the need to change employers.
- They tend to view employment in a larger firm as more secure – although that does not seem as powerful an argument as it was a few years ago!

As an aside, these attributes are even more strongly associated with the public services and the professional services sector which are most attractive to many graduates.

What you can offer

If you want to attract a graduate, what have you to offer? What kind of graduate is likely to want to work in a small enterprise? Graduates – like other people – differ one from another, and fortunately a lot of them are frankly a bit fed up with being cyphers in large organizations, i.e. universities and schools. Such graduates want challenge more than security, and an opportunity for identity and personal achievement rather than to be carefully shepherded through yet another learning programme. The key to success is to recruit the kind of graduate who is prepared to accept a large measure of personal responsibility and who is keen to **take part in building up a small business.** As you set about finding such a person, ensure that each step you take will help to bring about this match between the graduate's aims and abilities and expectations and what you have to offer by way of a challenging opportunity, and what you expect to get in return. Employing a graduate is not philanthropy, it is an investment. Like any major investment of time and money you should tackle this task in a business-like way.

Planning ahead The first thing to recognize is that if you intend to recruit a graduate straight from university, polytechnic or college you should plan a long way ahead. Although graduates are finding it difficult to get jobs, so it may be possible to find one to engage at short notice in the summer, the typical undergraduate starts looking for jobs in the spring before graduation. What is more to the point, perhaps, is the fact that many employers are actively recruiting in the universities at this point. Indeed many large employers have made a start much earlier by providing information and glossy brochures to the schools, the Careers Service, the university Careers Offices and so forth, and have advertisements and information in the various careers books and so on. Individually, small firms will not be able to compete with this – and indeed it is not necessary for you. It is, however, worth supporting the efforts of those who try to present the case for small firms to undergraduates, because this influences the climate in which decisions are made. Furthermore, you may well find that a modest investment of time in such activities will help you and may save you time and money when you want to recruit a graduate.

Thus if you are particularly interested in a high quality graduate, you should seek to recruit that individual and make an offer by Easter or thereabouts in the final year of the course.

The person concerned can start work for you in July, August or September. You can agree on that in advance. You will not know the class of degree, but by talking with the individual, and, with permission, with the tutors, you should be able to judge roughly what is expected. Do bear in mind that the honours classification system is not precise, particularly as between the upper and lower second-class bracket. In any case, unless there is a compelling reason to want a good honours graduate, the precise honours classification is not critical when it comes down to getting jobs done. If you want work, e.g. research in science or high technology, you must hire someone with at least an upper second-class honours degree. For research you are probably better off with someone who has obtained a higher degree by research (normally a PhD or MPhil, but you need to check this as the terminology at Master's degree level is not uniform).

As described in previous Units you will need to sketch out the job you will offer and draw up a simple person specification and an application form. A good plan would be to get this information down on two or three sides of A4 paper and send it with a covering note to two or three careers officers at universities and polytechnics. Do not forget the polytechnics. In general undergraduates at polytechnics are more likely to want to work in industry or commerce and to want to get down to a real job of work quickly, especially those who take courses involving periods of industrial experience. How do you choose which universities or polytechnics to contact?

What kind of graduate?

There are two important points to consider.

- Do you want a particular speciality? This will narrow the field. For example, only a few universities and polytechnics offer courses in Hotel and Catering Management, or in Estate Management or in Languages combined with Business Management.
- If you just want an intelligent person, why not approach the half-dozen which are within easy travelling distance of your home or office. This will make it easier for you to meet the careers people and perhaps some of the students.

It may not be easy for you to arrange a set of interviews over a short time span as described in Unit 17. It may be better for you to interview anyone you find, e.g. through the university or polytechnic careers services, who is interested, and when you consider you have found the right person, to make an offer. Remember that the undergraduates are actively job hunting and may be in touch with two or three other prospective employers. You may not be able to press for a very quick answer – indeed it is probably unwise to do this. The undergraduate might well accept under pressure and then recant when a better offer comes along. There is little you can do about that. On the other hand, if you have given the individual time to make a proper decision, given full information, arranged a visit to your firm and talks with your people, then the undergraduate is far less likely even to look for another position. In the few months up to the final examinations most sensible undergraduates want to concentrate on study with the knowledge that a job is in the bag.

Deciding what you want All this means that you must form a reasonably clear view of what you want, so that when you find the right person you are ready to act. If you want a particular discipline, then it is wise to involve in the interview someone who is an expert in the subject. You can assume a sound general coverage in the degree course, but you cannot assume that every degree in, say, chemistry or physics will cover adequately the particular area of chemistry or physics in which you are interested. Probe that in the interview if it is relevant. Apart from the need to check this technical matter, the primary aim of the interview should be to check out the match between your aims and expectations and those of the candidate, and the way in which your firm works.

If you and your senior people intend to spend a great deal of time coddling the newcomer, sending him or her on training courses and giving no authority or responsibility, that's one approach and it might appeal to some graduates. What is more likely is that the newcomer will be thrown in at the deep end, given little help or advice, a lot of responsibility and a modicum of authority. Make sure that the situation the graduate can expect when he or she arrives is clear. It will not deter the kind of person you are seeking. This means that the interview should be more of a chat, a sharing of ideas about what it is like to work in your firm and what the undergraduate is looking for in a job, and in an employer. How quickly can you establish a real two-way conversation, rather than an artificial question and answer situation? (See Unit 9.) Remember that in the event it will be the ability of the graduate to talk with and listen to you and your people that will be the touchstone of success. If the graduate is brilliant, but can't communicate with anyone in the firm, he or she is useless to you. You must share broadly the same values about people and industry.

The graduate arrives

When the graduate arrives at work, you or one of your people must go through the following routine:

- Explain the layout, introduce key people, make sure the newcomer understands the conditions of service and all the other points that make up a good induction.
- Be sure there is a proper working place and a real job to be done at the outset.
- Do not leave a new graduate floundering around looking for something to do. An induction checklist which can be handed to the individual is especially useful. It could have a list of items to be covered and, more significantly, a list of people to be seen, and topics to be covered in a brief chat in each case.
- Warn your people that the graduate is coming and ask each key person on the list to be prepared to spend a little time (say 15-20 minutes) telling the newcomer about their own job, how they fit in and about the work of any people who report to them.

There are obvious changes in moving from a place of learning to a place of production and business. There are new objectives, a different mix of people and a tighter control of time. The graduate will need to adjust and some simple help will speed up the acclimatization.

Feedback on progress The undergraduate's life is generally punctuated by examinations and other feedback on personal performance and progress. In your firm the output of the team is often more obvious and important, so that feedback on personal performance is different in character. You should ensure that the graduate is made aware, from time to time, of how you and perhaps one or two of your senior people view progress. This will help the graduate to meet your requirements – or perhaps to discuss them with you and agree on new aims and goals. Early on you should discuss the job description and some targets (as described previously), but do not be in too much of a hurry to revise the job description. This can be done after a few months, by which time the graduate should have gained sufficient grasp of the situation to make a really worthwhile contribution.

Reaction to questions One of the aspects of taking on a bright graduate is that before long he or she will be questioning some of your procedures and methods. Be careful how you react to that. Don't be too defensive. Be prepared to listen and to discuss the ideas presented. If they are clearly lacking in understanding, the discussion could be a valuable learning experience for the graduate. If the ideas put forward have merit, see if you can use them to improve the business. Do not reject them out of hand – or at least don't do that very often. No intelligent graduate will put up for long with having every idea rejected without discussion. They will either leave, or work without enthusiasm. If you hire people with brains you must expect them to use them.

Keep in touch

Graduates work best when they see where their efforts fit into the whole picture. This is where you, as a small firm, can score over some of the very large organizations:

- Take time to explain your overall business strategy – in simple terms if the graduate is not well-versed in business methods.
- In particular explain issues like fixed and variable costs, and cash flow.

- Don't make the mistake of equating intelligence with knowledge. Clever people can be ignorant if they have never been exposed to certain ideas and concepts. Many graduates are ignorant of financial matters. If they see the point about machine utilization and so forth, they will contribute more purposefully to your endeavours.

Giving real responsibility If you are too busy to spend some time with the graduate you may find it helpful to assign him or her to a senior member of your staff. This 'industrial tutor' would ensure that the graduate is properly inducted into the firm, has work to do and feedback on performance. You should expect the graduate to progress reasonably quickly and this can be helped along by providing a series of tasks, each one a bit more challenging than the previous one. As soon as you feel reasonably confident about it, give the graduate some real responsibility, including, where possible, responsibility for the work of one or two others. This sense of accountability – providing it is reasonable – is a very powerful way to develop leadership qualities. A new graduate might make one or two rather appalling blunders through inexperience. You must allow for this. Take comfort from the fact that graduates are likely to learn fast!

Reviewing progress It is wise to set up a formal review of the graduate's progress after six months and one year. Arrange a proper meeting for at least an hour, giving the graduate at least one, preferably two, weeks' notice. Urge him or her to make a note of things that have gone well and areas where the work needs to be improved. You can also jot down items of this kind. When you come together you can talk about the job (based on the description), any targets agreed and how well they have been achieved, and the specific points each of you have jotted down. Then look to the future, to the next six or twelve months:

- Agree on a revised job description and new targets.
- If there are areas that need improvement, agree on how this can be achieved.
- Does the graduate need improved knowledge or skills in some areas?

- How will this be done?
- Is it possible to rearrange responsibilities, procedures or work flows?

Let the conversation be truly two-way and constructive.

So far we have said little about postgraduate students taking research degrees or tutored courses. Unless your firm offers research services or aims to be at the leading edge of technological development you are unlikely to be particularly interested in people with PhD or MPhil degrees. But do not reject them out of hand. For the most part they will be exceptionally able in the intellectual sphere and if they can combine that with a common-sense approach to business and dealing with people, that is a powerful set of attributes.

Then there are a number of courses at Master's degree level where a graduate can deepen his or her knowledge, especially in technology and applied sciences. If you happen to need that specialization, people with these qualifications could be invaluable. There are also postgraduate courses in business and in specific areas of business, e.g. export marketing. If you want to strengthen the business side of your enterprise it might well be worth exploring the possibility of employing an MBA (Masters' Degree in Business Administration) or someone with similar qualifications.

Action Guidelines

1 What type of work in your firm, do you consider a young undergraduate could undertake?

2 Discuss your ideas with other business people who are already employing graduates.

3 Decide what discipline you will specify (if any) and what tasks you would give to a new graduate.

4 Decide how to monitor the progress of a recently appointed graduate.

5 If you want to recruit and interview a graduate for a job in a subject on which you are not an expert, what sort of help will you need, and where will you get it?

19

Helping the Newcomer

- What happens in the first few days can make a lasting impression on the newcomer. Attitudes and habits form quickly and change slowly.

- It may not seem like it to you, but there is really quite a lot to learn if the newcomer is to work well and feel 'at home' in the firm.

- It's a good idea to get the key things down on paper and then make sure that they are all covered in some way.

- Sound training need not be expensive and it is usually amply repaid in terms of people becoming effective quickly.

- It is most important to see that all health and safety matters are covered without delay.

The first day

First impressions really do make a difference, and in many ways what happens when a newcomer arrives can colour the working relationship for weeks or even months. Make sure the newcomer is expected by a few key people and that someone is clearly assigned the job of ensuring that the person has somewhere to sit and work, and that all the necessary information is given and introductions made. Nothing is worse, on the first day, than to gain the impression that you are not expected, that there is nowhere to sit or place to work, and no one has time to talk to you or to introduce you to the people with whom you will work.

The induction checklist In order to make sure that all the necessary items are covered it is wise to compile an induction

Figure 22 *Induction checklist*

- What does the newcomer need to know and at what stage?
- What is written down and what must be said?
- Who will give the information?
- Draw up your own list using the items below as a starting point.

Employment conditions	Pay rates, method of payment, payslips
	Overtime, holidays and other leave
	Sickness, absence and certificates
	Timekeeping and time recording methods
	Contract of employment
	Trade union membership
	Grievances and discipline procedures
	Terms of service (within first thirteen weeks)
Starting procedure	Documents, e.g. P45, birth certificate
	Medical examination, if required
	Protective clothing
	Introductions to key people
General information	Cloakrooms and washrooms
	Meals, breaks and eating places
	Welfare facilities and parking
	Smoking
	Security
	Purchases
Health and safety	Fire precautions and exits
	Action in case of fire or bomb threats
	Machine safety, tools and equipment
	Good housekeeping and hygiene
	Safety methods and first aid arrangements
The Firm	History and organization
	Products, services and markets
Personal training plan	

Note   It is useful to arrange an interview after a few months to see how the newcomer is getting on.

checklist (see Figure 22). A senior person who is starting work at your firm could be given this list and helped to work through it. For such a person the induction checklist could be accompanied by a prompt-list (see Figure 23), giving the names of some people in the firm who are important to the newcomer's role. The individual

Figure 23 *People prompt list*

(To the newcomer:) You should arrange to visit each of the people named below within your first week at the company if at all possible. If a particular individual is on leave, arrange to see him (or her) as soon as possible after the return to work. During your brief talk with them, find out what their role is in the firm, what they will expect of you in your job, and what help they can give you.

Name of person to be visited	Important items to be covered in your talk	Date and time of visit	Tick here after visit

would be asked to arrange to see each person on the list, to find out about their jobs and what they expect of the newcomer, and what help and information they can provide. The degree of formality in this depends on the size of your firm, but if you want senior people to become fully effective, this procedure is very useful. You must realize that in many jobs the ability to get in touch quickly with your opposite number elsewhere in the firm and to know what he or she expects of you and can give you, is more than half the battle.

For newcomers in less senior positions you will want to have one of your people work through the checklist with them. It seems a long list, but many of the items will take only a minute or two to explain, and others can be written down and handed to the person on the first day. Although most of this can be dealt with informally in the first day or two, it is important to ensure that all the key points are covered. It may not seem important to you to tell each newcomer something about the history of the firm, its products and so forth, but it is just this kind of information which helps people to gain a sense of belonging. If you have a small, family firm it won't take long, but it will be worthwhile. In many cases, if the foreman is given a schedule, this can be covered in the first morning. Make sure the newcomer reads the company discipline procedures and the safety rules.

Some firms, even small ones, sometimes have a little display of their goods or some photographs on an exhibition stand. This is useful for visitors and for new employees, does not cost much and takes up little space. (You may want to take it to trade exhibitions as well occasionally.) This does, of course, depend on the nature of your business, its products and its markets. Most people gain a measure of identity from the place where they work and this is reinforced if they understand clearly what goods or services it provides. If your firm makes parts rather than finished articles, it is worth getting some glossy photographs of the finished articles made by the firms that buy your components. Your employees can then say 'We make the headlamps for Mackey's Motorbikes' or whatever, or 'We make the ball-bearings for Concord'. This may seem a small thing, but it all helps to create an atmosphere where people feel they are doing something useful as part of a team (see Unit 3). Your aim, in these early days, is to encourage the newcomer to quickly feel a part of your enterprise.

Training

The last item on the induction checklist is the individual's training plan. This can be very simple or very elaborate depending on the individual and the job to be done. But whether it is short or long, do not neglect proper job training. Even if you recruit people with good skills, e.g. a trained secretary or an experienced turner, your firm has its own filing systems, component storage systems, work standards, recording systems and so forth. When you recruit young people, in particular, you will want to give them a sound, basic training in the job they have been recruited to do, but more than this you have a responsibility to give them wider experience and skills so that as your firm develops they will be able to learn and develop as well. If you have special machinery or special methods of packaging or fitting parts together into sub-assemblies or finished products, it is important to ensure that new employees are quickly able to work at a reasonable speed and to produce items of acceptable quality.

Taking the young people first, if you are taking on an apprentice or a young person on a traineeship you should ensure that:

- He or she is duly registered at the technical college and attends day-release classes.
- You appoint someone to act as a kind of 'industrial tutor', to take an interest in the youngster's progress, to talk about how studies are going and to see that training and experience on the job are worthwhile and properly carried through.
- Your training arrangements reach the required standards and that the youngster is adequately educated and trained to pass the required tests and examinations.
- Proper records are maintained.

If you intend to set about training young people in a serious way then you need a member of staff with the right skills and knowledge to do the training. These include technical ability and experience in a particular skill or specialism, but more is required. The trainer must have:

- Wide experience and knowledge, an awareness of the social situation of young people and an ability to communicate with them.
- The patience to tolerate variable standards of work or poor motivation at times, and the ability to help the youngster to higher achievements.
- High standards of personal behaviour and the ability to view and to deal with each young person as an individual.
- The ability to work well in a team and gain the co-operation of other workers in helping to train and develop the trainees.
- The ability to plan and implement training programmes and have the stamina to see them through.

You may not have a member of staff who has all these qualities in abundance but you should choose someone who corresponds as closely as possible to this specification and then give him or her every support in the task. Although instructional ability can help, the dominant need these days is for young people to learn how to find out for themselves by reading, watching, practising, under supervision at first, by asking questions and by accepting correction. An experienced worker who can encourage these activities and gain the respect and trust of the young people will be more effective than someone who can just give a good talk. At the workplace learning is a total experience of which the tutorial activity is but one part. Creating the situation where learning occurs and encouraging young people to make full use of the opportunities is the way to promote flexibility and personal development.

Let us consider some of the semi-skilled manual tasks that people do at work. Here there is no doubt at all that sound training is profitable in financial terms. By breaking the job down into a series of simple steps, and making sure that the trainee can master each of them, then gradually building these up into the total operation, finally practising to increase speed, produces fast, accurate workers. But in small firms there is often a need to change the operation in subtle ways, producing successive batches which are slightly different to preceding ones to meet changes in fashion, e.g. in the clothing trade, or to meet the needs of different customers, e.g. in the engineering industry. In this case, you may need to adopt a more subtle approach to training, and one which encourages more understanding and sensitivity on the part of the machine operators.

Flexibility

One way to develop flexibility is to allow people to 'discover' a lot of the work for themselves by breaking the task down as before, but then instead of demonstrating each step first, the tutor asks the trainee what he (or she) thinks should be done next. Then the trainee responds and is, perhaps, allowed to try things out and see what happens. Then they can be asked fresh questions about the results of their efforts and so on. The methods may sound cumbersome and it certainly takes more time to design the programme and patience and time to carry it through, but the result is someone who can now vary the sequence and settings of machines or whatever and tackle a variety of jobs without the need for fresh instruction each time. The initial investment in training design and implementation time will be adequately repaid if you have a need for flexible workers. You do need a competent trainer skilled in discovery methods, however, to make it work.

If you employ a graduate or a specialist, then to get full value for your salary bill, you will find it useful to spend time training them – mostly by coaching – to play their full and appropriate part in your firm's business. Some employers seem to think that because an employee arrives with a degree and/or a professional qualification, that person is a master of every aspect of the subject. That is simply not true. Therefore there may well be a need to provide that extra bit of training, e.g. by means of a short course at the local polytechnic or business school, or by a planned schedule of reading, to ensure that the newcomer is master of that bit of the subject which matters in your firm.

Furthermore, if you recruit someone, specialist or not, who is expected to supervise the work of others you should think carefully about the need for supervisory or management training at the appropriate level. There are courses which run for two or three days, useful for a short, sharp push in the right direction, and also longer courses on a part-time basis for supervisors. There are also correspondence-type courses, but since you can really only learn to manage by managing, you will need to give coaching support to anyone who takes a part-time or correspondence course. There are also a number of very useful techniques such as critical path analysis, time management, negotiating skills and quality assurance, which can be learned on short courses. If these are important in your business, then why not get your newcomer trained before he or she becomes so enmeshed in the job that two or three days out will be difficult.

Health and safety

Whatever job the newcomer has to do, it is vital that health and safety factors feature, as appropriate, in the training programme both in the induction and in the job training. In the written training schedule it is worth emphasizing safety points, e.g. using a different colour. See that they are kept up to date and that they are emphasized by the instructor. Pay particular attention to the operation of machinery, setting up procedures, starting and stopping, isolation procedures, cleaning down, test runs, use of guards, action to be taken if clothing, hair or parts of the body become caught up in the machines, and so forth. Ensure that the correct use of relevant fire appliances is covered and the wearing of protective clothing, including goggles and ear-muffs where appropriate.

Safe working practices are as much a matter of attitude as of procedures. This means that you and other managers must set a clear example, and constantly emphasize their importance. This must extend to good housekeeping, proper stacking of materials and cartons, cleaning up spillages and a complete ban on dangerous 'horse-play' and suchlike. Be particularly wary of unseen dangers: poisonous fumes, X-rays, micro-organisms and so forth. Here, above all, correct attitudes and procedures must be inculcated from the very first moment that the newcomer enters the danger zone.

Action Guidelines

1 Make a note of the key points in an induction programme for newcomers to your firm.

2 If you expect a newcomer, how will you cover these key points? Who will be responsible for seeing that the induction training is carried out properly?

3 If you have a newcomer, how will you ensure that he or she is making satisfactory progress?

4 If you have employed a person who is a specialist in a discipline you are not familiar with, how will you satisfy yourself that he or she is making a real contribution to the firm?

5 To what extent do you intend to inform newcomers about the overall policy of the firm, its history and its prospects? How will you get this message across?

20
Retirement, Redundancy and Resignation

- For many people a job is an identity, so that the loss of a job is far more than the loss of livelihood.
- If you treat people in a compassionate way when they come to leave, not only will you help them, it will rub off in benefits to the firm in the positive attitudes of the workers who remain.
- Many of these considerations apply when people resign. If you have a lot of resignations you should look into this.
- If you consider the time has come to make people redundant, think again. People are more versatile and resilient than we often imagine. Consider other possibilities.
- If you really have to do it, remember that people take time to adjust to change and do all you can to help them cope with it.
- Remember that how you handle this will have a big effect on the workers who remain with you.

Retirement

We discussed dismissal earlier, and in this Unit we shall consider other reasons why people leave and how these situations should be managed. When someone reaches retirement age, or decides to retire a little earlier (for health reasons for example) they are approaching a serious crisis in their lives. For many people working life gives them a great deal more than wages. It gives them an identity and a social environment. To some extent that identity can often be carried into retirement: 'I used to be a storekeeper at Jackson's' you hear people say. It helps to establish who they are. Then again, in most jobs there is an element of stability and security in meeting and talking to people each day. There is also a reason to get up and go out each day. Thus the loss of a job is far more than a dramatic reduction in income.

Although you may have no formal responsibility for people once they have retired, the way you treat such people will be noted by your other employees and this will affect their attitude to you. Many firms take active steps to encourage employees to prepare for retirement, and to get advice on how to manage their financial affairs, how to manage their new-found time and how to deal with their social lives. If you want to do this, there is a Pre-Retirement Association which can give you a lot of helpful advice, leaflets, etc. There are also short courses (a few days) where people can get advice on how to cope with the various problems associated with retirement and seek the advice of experts. These courses are most helpful several months ahead of the retirement date.

You may wish to organize an occasion to present a gift to the person who is retiring and serve some drinks and light refreshment. Organizations differ in the way these functions are run, who pays, and so forth, but it is a good custom to have an occasion where you say a few words of thanks to the retiring person, perhaps mentioning a few highlights or humorous events in his working life at your firm. Then you can convey the good wishes of yourself and your colleagues and present the gift. You must use your own judgement in such cases.

The state pension scheme is not very generous, and if your company is well established you might approach two or three of the insurance companies who specialize in these matters and arrange a company scheme for your employees. This is a highly technical business and you should take professional advice.

Resignations

What do you do when people resign? To a large extent this depends on the circumstances. If you have a high labour turnover and people leave after a few weeks or months, you should try to have a brief word with them to see if you can find out why they have resigned. You must remember that when you ask someone why they are leaving, they are unlikely to give you the whole answer. There will be many quite obvious and sound reasons for moving on which need not give you cause for concern. However, if you find that people are leaving because your wage levels are considered too low, or your working conditions poor, or the social atmosphere is hostile, then perhaps you need to consider these issues more seriously. You may have people leaving because they feel they are not told clearly enough what to do or that they have not been trained properly for the job, or that they feel the work practices are unsafe. These are all issues that you must consider carefully and deal with if there are any grounds at all in them.

Whatever reason is given for the resignation (if any) it is generally a good idea to try to keep the relationship on a friendly basis. You might want to re-engage the person later, and in any case you don't want too many people walking about saying you are a terrible employer! It is not usual to have farewell parties for people who have not been with the firm very long. Some firms have an understanding that special events and collections are normal only for people who have been with the firm for more than two years. Even then you find occasionally that folk will collect for an individual who has been particularly popular and helpful. There are no hard and fast rules about this, but as an employer you should endeavour to be fair in the way you involve yourself in these arrangements.

When someone leaves under happy circumstances, e.g. to get married and move away with the spouse, or to move to an exalted position or to fulfil an ambition, the farewell presentation party can often help to improve relationships between people in the firm. It is an opportunity to chat informally with other people without the constraints and concerns of work. It can enable you to get to know some of your people in a different context.

Redundancy

To turn our attention to less happy themes, you may be in the unfortunate position of having to declare people redundant. The term 'redundancy' means that a job disappears, and this may arise in several different ways. The business may close down completely – when all the jobs are lost. One facet of the business may be in decline so that you will need less people with particular skills. You may wish to introduce new machinery or working methods which will require less people to achieve the output which you need to satisfy the market. In certain circumstances people who have been laid off or kept on short-time may be considered redundant.

Alternatives You must be clear about the fact that if you replace one employee by another who is doing the same job, the replaced employee is not redundant – because no job has disappeared. Similarly, an employee who is dismissed for inefficiency, unsuitability, ill health or misbehaviour cannot be considered as redundant. These considerations are particularly important in relation to entitlement to redundancy pay, and to your ability as an employer to claim any rebate from the Government. You should refer to the current state of the law on these matters, and it is wise to notify the Department of Employment, and the local Jobcentre or Employment Exchange if you are about to make some people redundant. You have a legal obligation to notify the Department if you propose to make ten or more people redundant.

Before taking the final decision to make people redundant you should talk it over with the union representative (if any) or your senior colleagues. Are you quite sure there is no other alternative? Let us consider the disappearance of certain kinds of jobs because of changes in technology, procedures or market demand. If different jobs are being created somewhere in your firm, is there any possibility at all that the workers you are about to declare redundant could be retrained to do the new jobs? Have you considered a more ambitious scheme of moving some of the workers you intend to retain into the new jobs and to retrain the possibly redundant workers into these existing jobs? You may find this easier in terms of training, although it does involve more reallocation of jobs.

Another idea that has been used occasionally is to become more aggressive in your marketing and selling operation. Could you retrain some of the redundant workers as salesmen, thereby increasing your market share, creating more work for the people who produce your goods or provide your services at the firm? Of course, some of your workers will not be suitable for the role of sales people. Many small firms have a much greater potential market than they realize, and it is often a viable proposition to go out and get more business. There is often an untapped market overseas, and with a little help you may be able to move into these areas. This book is not about marketing and selling, but a fresh thrust in this direction should be seriously considered by any employer whose need for employees is decreasing. Another reason for a decline in business is cash flow and lack of investment. Once again such matters are outside the scope of this book (but see **How to Manage Money** in this series) but do seek sound professional advice before you give up hope.

The last resort If we assume that all your discussions and considerations of alternative strategies come to nought, you must inform people that there will be redundancies. Do not forget that as soon as the news is out, everybody in the firm is likely to feel insecure. This kind of news affects everyone, not just the people who will be made redundant. The typical reactions will, at first, be **shock** and **disbelief**. Even if people had sensed that all was not well in the firm, the mention of redundancy will add an immediacy and an urgency to their concerns. They will wonder who will be next and how long their own jobs will be secure. Good morale will be difficult to maintain. Many people may feel a strange sense of **guilt**, wondering whether there was something they should have done to prevent this calamity. Many of these feelings will seem irrational, but they are real. We have noted before that when people feel threatened they react by **flight or fight**. Some of your people will be tempted to get out fast and look for jobs with employers who seem more secure. Others will feel resentful and look for someone to blame for the decline in the business. All these feelings and emotions will come to the surface and interfere with the smooth running of the firm – although many of the minor irritations people display will seem quite unconnected with the real issues.

Why have we mentioned all this about people's feelings? Because you need to know what is going on if you hope to manage the situation. The key to managing in this situation is to do all you can to deal with the four reactions outlined above – shock, disbelief,

Figure 24 *Reaction to redundancy announcement*

People's reaction	Helpful action
Shock	Give as much notice as you can.
Disbelief	Talk with people about alternatives.
Guilt	Help people understand why it has become necessary.
Flight/fight	Be honest with people about prospects for the firm and their jobs.
Thinking through	Help people to see what their future might hold.
Coping	Do all you can to help those who leave to find alternative employment.

guilt and the flight/fight reaction (see Figure 24). What is happening to the people in the firm as a whole is greatly magnified in the case of those who are actually facing redundancy.

You therefore have two groups of people to think about, those who will be leaving as redundant and those who, hopefully, will remain behind and continue to work for you. If you can help people through these first four stages, then they will be able to think through what is happening and likely to happen, and to cope with it. This is where your powers of leadership will be called into play to the full.

Do not forget that you are likely to suffer some of the same emotions yourself – especially the feeling of guilt. Don't be tempted to run away from the problem, and don't waste much time on finding people to blame. Get down to dealing with the problem. Your people will be looking to you for leadership. What can you do in practical terms?

• Give people as much notice as possible that there are serious problems ahead. People generally find it easier to think clearly about problems in the future than about the crises that suddenly confront them. The only snag with revealing your hand too early is that it extends the period of uncertainty, but on balance, the sooner the better. You can yourself approach the problem more quietly and give the impression that you are in control. If you do it all in a rush, people will assume that you were taken by surprise and have lost your grip as a manager.

- Get discussions going on alternative courses of action so that by the time you have to make decisions people come to realize that there really are no other viable courses of action. (Naturally, if other possibilities become feasible as a result of these discussions you will wish to consider them very carefully.) Discussions like this also help people to understand the reasons for the dismissals and reduces the likelihood that they will feel guilty and look for scapegoats to put the blame on. There is some advice about getting discussions going in Unit 9.

If you want to continue running a well motivated team after the dust has settled you should:

- Be honest with people all through the exercise.
- Be honest, in particular about the prospects for the firm and the likely position of each of your people.
- Help people to see what the future is likely to hold for them.
- Without disclosing important business secrets, let people know what the areas of uncertainty are, as well as those things you are sure about.
- Do your utmost to help the people who must leave to find alternative employment.
- If you can see far enough ahead and help these people get jobs elsewhere before you need to dismiss them, your reputation and esteem as an employer will be high.

Action Guidelines

1 If you are unfortunate enough to be in the position where you must reduce the number of people you employ, what is the sequence of events leading up to the departure of those you make redundant. You may find the following headings useful:
   Preliminary planning
   Consultations
   Financial implications – redundancy payments
   Notification to Department of Employment
   Help to find other employment.

2 In a redundancy situation, what actions can be taken to minimize the dislocation and upset caused to your employees and how can you maintain the morale of your team?

3 What arguments will you use to convince your people and the trade union or staff representative that you really must make people redundant?

21
Helping People Improve

- Developing people is not only necessary if the work is to be done properly, it also gives a sense of confidence and enhances motivation.
- Developing people should go hand in hand with the development of your firm, and this means that the learning that takes place should largely be related to the operation of the enterprise.
- Development goes beyond just training people for the jobs to be done. It means challenging people to help you create the future, looking at your markets, materials and methods.
- You can do a lot yourself as a coach, as development can be way of life, rather than something extra to the way the firm operates.

Developing people

If you have a stable workforce and all your people have been trained to do their jobs properly, don't think that is the end of it. Today, more than ever, the world refuses to stand still, and we must also keep on the move. Furthermore, people themselves tend to mature and develop, and it will often be wasting talent to have them doing the same things in the same way for years on end. Younger people and professional people (specialists), in particular will want to see some progress and changes in their working lives, and if you want to maintain enthusiasm and motivation you will need to take account of this in your planning and use of people. When a newcomer joins the firm, unless he or she is a straight replacement, there will be changes in the roles of other people. This will most likely have training and people-development implications.

Figure 25 *Changes and learning needs*

The ultimate question in each case is 'what are the implications for my people?'. This list is intended to provoke thought. It is not exhaustive.

Aspect of change	Possible implications
Market-place	
• Is the market for my goods or services expanding? Will this continue?	• Do I need more staff, or more productive methods? What training will staff need?
• Is the market demand changing? Do I need to introduce new products or shift the balance of my current range?	• Do I need fresh designs and more creativity from my people? Do I need more flexibility from my staff, or some new skills?
Materials and methods	
• Should I be using different raw materials, either because of quality, price or availability?	• Will this mean that methods need to be modified? Can my people do the modifications? Can they use the new kind of material, or are new skills needed?
• Should I be introducing new methods, new technology, e.g. robotics, computers or word processors?	• Will my people need to be trained to use new machines and new methods?
People	
• Should I encourage people to develop their skills and to accept more responsibility?	• Will some training be required to help forward the process of people development?
• Should I take into account people's desire to be consulted and more involved in decisions?	• Will I need to see they are trained to understand the issues and to be able to contribute constructively?

Most of the changes you will have to accommodate will fall under one of three headings, the market-place, materials and methods, and people (see Figure 25). **If you want to stay in business you will have to meet the needs of the market-place.** You probably take care of this yourself to a large extent. If not, you must ensure that one of your people does, and that they really know what they are doing. If the market for your goods and services dries up, you are out of business. Your own expertise and that of the one or two people who may work with you on this are absolutely crucial to your long-term survival. Do not neglect training here.

If we can assume that you have correctly identified a trend in your markets, how do you propose to respond? If it merely involves expanding production of some goods and contraction elsewhere, you have the problem of redeploying some people. You will minimize disruption and uncertainty by sharing with your people both the reasons for the change and the way in which you intend to cope with it. Furthermore, if you can attend to the retraining requirements ahead of time you will avoid giving the impression of panic and mismanagement. If you consider that there is a need for new products or services, you have a design problem. If you consider that a few of your people could probably come up with sensible answers, why not form a small project group. Remember what we have said elsewhere about people working together (see Unit 5 and the Appendix).

Creative groups

- A creative group needs special leadership. It is no use at all trying to run it like a committee.
- A creative group must be helped to work in a much freer fashion.

A good way to work is to begin by making sure, through discussion, that everybody really understands the problem. In this exploratory stage let people ask the 'idiot' question. Don't discourage any question, even if it seems irrelevant. Use this session to throw up all the issues that have to be tackled. You may well find that you will need more information, e.g. about the number of potential customers for your proposed products, about the quality and price of competitors' items and so forth, or about the availability and cost of new kinds of raw materials. One way to generate new ideas is to employ the 'brainstorming' technique described in Unit 9 in your project group meeting.

The procedure described above is also just one kind of project group that you might form. Bear in mind that participation in project groups of this kind not only makes for better solutions to problems, it has two very important side effects. The people involved are much more committed to the solution and determined to see it succeed. Secondly, the experience helps people to develop their own capabilities, not only by doing something challenging, but also by learning from each other. If they have to go outside the group for information, then this provides further opportunities for learning. The power of the project group in helping people to develop and to work together is so great that it can be used quite deliberately for this purpose. For example you might include in the group someone whose contribution, though real, is unlikely to be outstanding. But the main purpose of this person's inclusion is personal development. (It will not help development if the person has nothing to contribute.)

Skills for new tasks

New products and services If you do decide to make a new product or to offer a new service there will be implications for the skills and knowledge of your staff. But this can also arise from changes in the cost or availability of the raw materials you use, or through a deterioration in quality. This may mean that you have to cope with tougher or more fragile materials, for example, which may mean different machine settings or different manufacturing methods. Then again your methods may have to change in the office, for example, because of changes in the law. Changes in the taxation system, in safety requirements (in the factory or for the customer) may mean that procedures must be changed. It is all too easy to overlook the training implications. Do not forget that sometimes a relatively small change may be better accommodated by reviewing procedures overall. A succession of minor modifications to procedures can easily produce a nightmare system if you do not keep your eye on this.

Technological developments It is also important to keep abreast of technological developments. These can influence the nature of the product or services you provide, the way in which products are designed, the way items are produced and packaged and the way information is handled. You cannot afford to neglect these developments and yet it is never easy to know just the right moment to invest in sophisticated new gadgets, or to upgrade your products and services. We have mentioned elsewhere that people are naturally suspicious of the unknown and need to be informed and consulted about ensuring that they are properly trained to use new technical gadgets safely. If people quickly master new pieces of equipment, their confidence is reflected in their morale and motivation to work. If their early experience is failure and mistakes, you could have problems for a long time, as people do not trust either the machine or their own ability to use it. So-called 'teething' troubles caused by mismanagement and lack of training are often far more costly than we realize.

The firm's needs You may be tempted to scoff at the idea of simply helping people develop their skills without reference to the specific needs of your firm. Indeed it may be inappropriate in your particular situation. But there are many firms where the health and growth of the enterprise is enhanced by having healthy 'growing' people around – growing in the sense of increasing their knowledge and skills, becoming more mature and sound in their judgements. Indeed, as we move further into the age of uncertainty and change, flexibility and maturity in a workforce will be far more valuable than a narrow competence in the specific tasks in the enterprise where they work. For this reason companies are prepared to take the risk of losing some good people (who might 'outgrow' the opportunities in the firm) by encouraging their personal development. The gain is a highly motivated, thrusting group of people. You must judge for yourself how far it is appropriate for you to go down this road.

Who needs training?

If you have identified the changes taking place, you must now consider clearly the people affected and how they are affected (see Figure 26). Think about all the secondary effects of change.

Example 1 If you intend to introduce a faster machine making engine parts, what affect will this have on the craftsman operating the machine, the person who is responsible for supplying raw materials, the individual who will receive the completed components and the foreman who must co-ordinate all this.

- Will there be different storage problems? How will this be dealt with?
- Will this new machine feed two paint shops instead of one?
- How will the material be shifted around, and who will do it?
- Who will maintain the machine routinely and how will this person be trained?

Example 2 If you purchase a word processor/computer:
- Who will operate it?
- Who will program it and who will use the computer print-out of the accounts?
- If this means that your typist will have more spare time (because less time will be spent typing) how will this be used?
- If she or he takes work over from someone else, say an accounts clerk, what new work will the latter person have?

This sounds daunting, but as you run down the list you will find a lot of the answers are not difficult at all, and you can deal with many of the training problems, in-house, quite easily. Training is often undertaken by the manufacturers who provide new machines, particularly in the computer field. But beware, good as this training may be, it is unlikely to be enough to ensure that you get full value from the investment. The more you know about the capabilities of new technology, the more likely you are to be able to use it imaginatively for the good of your business.

Specific skills From time to time you may find that one of your people needs a specific skill or updating in knowledge, e.g. in new legislation, new accounting methods, new safety procedures, or perhaps in some quite ordinary area like route planning, critical path analysis or first aid. You should shop around for short courses offered by the local college, professional bodies and other training

Figure 26 *People, change and training*

Changes identified	*People involved*	*Training need/method*
(List here the changes you have identified)	(List here each of the people involved in implementing the change and living with it afterwards)	(List here, for each person named, what is their need for training and how you propose to deal with it)

organizations. In many cases timely courses of this kind can be of great help.

Cost When you come to count the cost of training you may be discouraged. A good antidote to this is to consider the cost of not training. What would it be like if your miller or turner spent half the morning trying to set up the machine, or if your secretary used only one finger of each hand for typing. Suppose your accounts clerk put half the figures in the wrong columns. That's silly, you might say. But it only sounds silly because the results of not training are obvious. If you think about it, there is often much time and money wasted in firms because people don't really know how to do their jobs properly. It is much more difficult to prove when you're dealing with managers and supervisors, because poor decisions are less obvious, but often these are the mistakes that ruin the firm. Sound training really pays, however difficult it may be to prove in money terms, especially at senior levels.

Keeping records

You will need to keep some records about your staff. In essence you must comply with certain legal requirements, relating to tax and national insurance, but you will want to go beyond this. Do not, however, make your recording system unduly cumbersome. To begin with you will obviously need the name and address of the person concerned, the date of birth and the next of kin (in case of an accident or illness at work). Make sure you have a way of keeping the address up to date. You will need to complete a Deductions Working Sheet, and alongside this you will need an ongoing record of attendance, overtime, absences due to sickness and so forth, and of how wages are made up.

It is also a good idea to keep a record which shows the **qualifications**, **experience** and **abilities** of the individual, and this can be supplemented by a note of any training courses attended. If you employ a graduate you might find it helpful to keep a note of any reviews of performance you have and the key points which arise in your discussions. Large firms have formal appraisal systems for staff, but since this is not commonplace in small firms, procedures are not discussed here. Clearly, if any member of staff is involved in grievance or disciplinary procedures, you must keep full and careful notes at each step in the proceedings. These may be needed as evidence later if things go badly wrong. You will find it useful to have a folder for each member of staff and to keep in it the basic information, correspondence and so forth.

Quite apart from the formal training we have discussed, it is wise to cultivate an atmosphere where people feel keen to learn and to improve, and where senior people feel a responsibility to help and encourage those who work for them.

- If someone admits they need to learn something, this is not ridiculed or regarded as some kind of admission of failure. It should be seized upon as a positive indication that the person concerned wants to do a better job.
- You should avoid saying things like: 'I had to learn this the hard way, so should these young people!'. It does not help anyone.
- Don't be afraid that your people will know too much. The most successful managers are those who can get really clever people around them and then work with and through them to achieve results.

Once or twice we have mentioned coaching, and your aim should be to create a situation in which there is both the time, the inclination and the acceptance of the need for senior staff to spend time working through difficult problems and new ideas with their people. Naturally, you will have to set the example, since actions speak louder than words here. As your top people find you working with them in a positive and constructive way, so they will feel disposed to give the same kind of help to their subordinates.

Action Guidelines

1 Review your attitude to training. Do you pay enough attention to training people to do their jobs properly?

2 Make a rough estimate of what you spend on training – salaries, administration, cost of courses and so on. Then make a rough estimate of the cost of low productivity, errors in the office, machine breakdowns and suchlike.

3 Select some key staff members and consider whether they are trained to peak efficiency. If not, what kind of coaching or training will you give them?

4 Are there some particular areas where you feel your senior group of people could do with more understanding, e.g. estimating, cost control, profitability? What steps can you take to deal with this?

22
Keeping Ahead with People

- Management is learned by managing and improving on the job. You will need to keep in mind the tasks that you and your people must achieve if your firm is to be successful.
- Then you will need to have regard to the way individuals are working and how they perform together.
- To maintain momentum, look ahead and prepare your people for the future.
- Recognize your own strengths and weaknesses so that you may improve your performance and leadership qualities.

The craft

Managing people is a craft, not a science. It is something you can learn only by doing it and by practising and improving on the job. Furthermore, the situation is constantly changing and so are the people. Some of these changes will be slow and almost imperceptible, others may be sudden and dramatic. You will find that you change as you mature and as you gain experience and knowledge. The effective manager will accordingly be sensitive to these matters and gradually adjust his or her style of management to deal with new situations, and with people whose abilities and aspirations are changing. For the most part, business is a constant battle for survival, let alone success, and we need to get all our people working alongside us, sharing many of our aims and ambitions for the firm, and playing their respective parts competently, constructively and in collaboration with others.

Of the many areas we have discussed, four ideas are worthy of emphasis.

- The first idea is that of TASK: what is it that you and your people have to achieve?
- Secondly there is the TEAM, the group of people who must pull it off.
- Thirdly there are the INDIVIDUALS, the members of the work group, the people who work in the firm, each with different needs and making different contributions to both the tasks of the enterprise, and to the interactions between people at work.
- Lastly, there is the LEADER, you – upon whom it all ultimately depends.

Key tasks

From time to time you will need to review the business you are in and the tasks you undertake. You must take into account the strengths and weaknesses of your firm (and its people), the environment as it affects the business, the opportunities you can see as well as any actual or potential threats (like legislation which might affect your products, or new competitors who might reduce your ability to sell your wares). You must judge to what extent you involve members of your team in decisions about the overall direction of the firm. They should certainly be involved in considering the tasks they will be expected to perform, any targets you set and any monitoring methods you use. It is important to ensure that everyone knows what is expected of him or her.

- You will need to look ahead, to establish priorities, and to agree standards of workmanship.
- You must ensure that individual members of the team are competent to do what is required, and to arrange for training, coaching or other learning experiences as appropriate, e.g. visits to exhibitions, projects, a spell in a different job.

- You will need to see that people relate effectively to each others, workwise, and that there are no breakdowns in communication to undermine efficiency.
- You will want to delegate decisions as appropriate and ensure follow-up to see that they are carried through.
- You will also need to see that some people are not kept idle whilst others are toiling away, and that you have some way of ensuring that orders are met on time and that quality is maintained.

Although numerical targets may be appropriate in many ways, do bear in mind that they are not always the answer. Moreover, if you are not very careful, numerical targets can deflect attention away from more critical areas of performance. For the most part these are TASK-centred considerations, focusing on what needs to be achieved and what methods should be used.

Key people

In considering the motivation and effectiveness of the **team** and the **individual** members of it, you will need to consider your own management style and the way in which you communicate with your people. Remember that although you can attract people to a job through good wages, and encourage them through good working conditions, real motivation comes through a sense of achievement and involvement in something worthwhile. This means that you must make time and put real effort into making sure that you tell your people what is going on, and is likely to happen – not merely those bits that need to concern them because of their jobs, but the broader picture, so that they can see where their efforts fit into the total pattern of the firm's activity and aims. This is particularly important in respect of your key people and your top team. But the information should flow not merely downwards, but upwards, sideways and perhaps 'diagonally' as well. You should encourage people to share their ideas about the firm and its tasks with you and with each other. This communication is not merely to establish understanding at the intellectual level, but deeper still. It is to get people to understand why each person views things slightly differently, why decisions have to take into account other people's objectives and perspectives. How does the sales manager view this problem, or the production manager or the engineering maintenance manager and so forth. TEAM work is more than a group of people each doing a job linked to the others. It means a responsiveness which involves considering how your own actions and decisions, as a team member, will make life easier, or more difficult, for another team member.

Motivation Since motivation can come from job content you will want to keep an eye on this:

- Are people finding their jobs satisfying?
- Should you be doing more to give people variety, or more 'complete' jobs to do?

Don't forget that if you enrich one person's job you are in danger of making someone else's less rich. Of course, if you or your senior people have plenty to do – that's usually the case – you should not find it difficult to delegate more work and responsibility to others. This will enrich their jobs. People also derive satisfaction from being 'in the know' and being consulted. Don't forget this powerful method of rewarding people. Workers also welcome sincere and sensible praise for jobs well done, and they are amenable to constructive criticism mixed in with such praise.

Reviewing progress Another way to help build and maintain the team is to hold periodic reviews of progress and aims for the future. In such sessions it is important to review successes and failures and to learn from these experiences. If things are going well it is not too difficult to keep people happy and well-motivated. If your market is expanding and your machinery and people are performing well you are unlikely to have morale problems. But what happens when you run into trouble? This is where your efforts at leadership and team building will count. When a badly led group of people runs into trouble, the members start to blame each other and to look for scapegoats. When a well-led team faces trouble, they encourage each other and look for solutions. We have indicated earlier some of the steps you can take when you see trouble brewing. These steps amount to treating people like adults, giving them time to adjust and giving them compass bearings so that they have at least some idea where they are heading.

A good manager does not neglect the individual members of his or her team. Each one counts. This is not merely a question of support when things go wrong for that person, it is a question of seeing that people have satisfying work to do, feel competent and know that their efforts are recognized. One member of the team who goes off the boil and loses confidence or enthusiasm will start to have an effect on the others. They will either follow this example (if your leadership is poor) or support that person, hiding the problem (if they consider you will not be helpful) or they will support that person and seek your help, so that as a team you can do something positive and constructive about it.

The future

Since one of the main responsibilities of a leader is to point the way ahead, when you foresee change on the horizon you must decide how to prepare your people for it, how to inform them and how to involve them in the planning and preparations for it. In many ways the extent to which you feel confident to involve people in such matters, and the way in which they respond to this, will be a most important indicator of how far you have become a good manager. Apart from external factors, the success of your firm is largely dependent on the ability and enthusiasm of your people. Their competence and keenness depends on you, your leadership and the way you manage them.

Appendix

The Way People Contribute to Meetings

When a group of people meet together to perform a task, a number of personal interactions take place, both verbal and non-verbal. In some cases the 'process' of interaction is productive, i.e. it helps the group to achieve its goals efficiently.

This is a large subject but there are some simple tools you can use to begin to understand what is actually happening. It is a short step from this to improving the way your group works.

The simplest thing you can do is to make a note each time someone speaks. This can be done using Figure A. Put a mark each time Helmut speaks and so forth, using the five-bar gate method to aid adding up the totals later.

When you come to look at the results, look at high scores – is that person hogging the conversation? Look at low scores and consider whether that person should be encouraged to say more. If you like, you can put more marks down as people speak longer, so that you don't confuse a few long speeches (low score) with non-contributors. Used in this way the technique is not scientific, but it can give you some clues. Its main value is the way it gets you to look at what people are contributing rather than just being concerned with the progress the group as a whole is making.

A more difficult technique is to try to analyse what kind of contribution each person makes. You can use a five-category system for this as in

Figure A   Totals

Helmut	⊬⊬⊬ //	7
Carl	//	2
Jane	⊬⊬⊬ ⊬⊬⊬	10
Joe	⊬⊬⊬ /	6

Figure B

	Total
Agreeing	
Disagreeing	
Building	
Questioning	
Proposing	

Figure B. You will not be able to fit everything neatly into one of these five categories, but don't worry too much about that. Have a go, and you will begin to learn a lot about how people – your people – behave in the group.

Agreeing and *Disagreeing* are pretty straightforward. *Building* is when people say things which build on or carry forward ideas which are discussed at the time. This is more positive than simple agreement with what is being said. *Proposing* is when someone puts forward quite new ideas, which may well cut across what is being said by others. *Questioning* is when people request clarification of the ideas being discussed. Destructive questions should be classified as *Disagreeing*. At first you may be content with just recording the kind of contributions. With practice you may be able to note the kind of contribution each person makes.

There is no need to become very sophisticated about all this, but using these techniques does help you to become more aware of 'process' issues.

Index

ability, 14-18, 84
agenda, 106
analysis, diary, 29
  mistakes, 87
  misunderstanding, 95-103
  application form 166-7

brainstorming, 104
briefing meetings, 104
business, nature of, 38

change, coping with, 49
  introducing, 50
  preparing for, 51, 210-11
  technology, 140-8
circulars, 115
clarity, 109
colour, 45
communication, 3
confidence building, 131
consultation, 52-56
  preparing for, 55
control, 78-79
coping with crises, 35
  with change, 109
correcting people, 82, 87
correction, positive, 82

deadlines, 25
decision-making, 36, 54, 156
decoration, 45-46
describing jobs, 22-26
developing people, 209-17
diary analysis, 29
disabled people, 134-9
discipline, 90
discouragement, 76-77
discrimination, 118, 122-123

encouragement, 70-77
  control, 78-79
  information, 79
  lack of, 86
  praise, 78
enthusiasm, 72
entrepreneurs, 154
environment, 41, 47
equipment, 137-8, 140-8
evaluation, job, 22
expectation, 128

fear, of change, 51
fire risk, 24, 42, 138-9

groups, 33-39, 103-107
  creative, 211
  mixed age, 129

health and safety, 24-5, 41, 138-9, 199
hearing, 92
hiring people, 158

induction, 192-3
information, 51, 79, 113
  lack of, 86
  young people, 128-9
instruction, job 130
interviews, formal, 88
  recruitment, 166-7
  specialist, 176-7

job description, 22-26, 160-1
  evaluation, 22
  instruction, 130
joint decision-making, 54

key contacts, 27-29
  people, 14, 27
  tasks, 220-1

layout, 42
leadership, 150-6
letter-writing, 110-115
light, 44
listening, 92-107
location, 47-48, 74
loyalty, 130, 134

management style, 74, 150-6, 218-9
man in charge, 120
meetings, 103-107
  briefing, 104
  minutes, 107
minutes, 107
misbehaviour, 90
mistakes, 83, 86, 87
misunderstanding, 95-103
mixed age group, 129
motivation, 14-18, 70-81, 151, 222

negotiation, 53-55
  objectives, 57-58
  meetings, 59-60
  preparation for, 55
noise, 44

opposite sex, 118-124
organization chart, 16

patience, 127
positive correction, 82
  motivation, 18
potential, 14-18
praise, 78
premises, 40-6, 136-7
problem solving, 35

records, 216-7
recruitment, 146, 158-169
  graduates, 182-190
  specialists, 170-180
  young people, 126-133

redundancy, 146, 203-207
resignations, 202
responsibility, 86
retirements, 201-2
reviewing progress, 104, 222-3
  graduates, 189
  situations, 102
  targets, 66
  technology, 148

safety, 24-5, 41, 138-9
sales letters 116
security, 46-47
selection criteria, 163, 172-7, 186-7
self-image, 154-5
sex, opposite, 118-124
sexual harassment, 120
social event, 79
space, 44
stress, 84-86

talking, 92-107
targets, 62-69
  clarity, 63
  levels, 62
  quality, 63
  reviewing, 66-69
  setting, 65-66
teamwork, 19, 32-39
  improving, 37
  rating, 34
  relationships, 19
technology, 140-8, 212-3
tidiness, 44
time, use of, 29
timekeeping, 132
trade unions, 54
training, 196-199, 213-6

woman in charge, 121
words, choice of, 113
writing, 109

young people, 126-133
  disabled, 137
Youth Training Scheme, 133

Starting the business. Here's how to keep i

The key to keeping your business going is to keep it growing. That means you need more people to help you, bigger premises, more customers and maybe even new products. And as your company grows, your accounts get more complex and less understandable. Suddenly you small business isn't so small any more, and it's hard to keep control.

The only way to cope is to call in the experts. The new *Building Your Business* series is a unique collection of tips and techniques from top business consultants who have already experienced *and solved* the problems you're facing now. Each book is packed with practical business know-how to help *you* keep *your* business going and growing.

BUILDING YOUR BUSINESS

Manage Money

A SUNDAY TELEGRAPH guide

- 20 questions to test your knowledge of money matters in your business
- how to control your working capital, how to improve your cash flow and how to do a cash flow forecast
- 14 ways of controlling costs
- how to make better business decisions through sound money management

G.D. Donleavy and M. Metcalfe

* how to answer your bank manager's questions
* 14 ways to control your costs
* how to do a cash flow forecast
* how good money management helps you make better business decisions

* how to keep your customers satisfied
* all you need to know about market research, pricing, advertising, developing new products and exporting
* how to sell the *sizzle* not the sausage
* the information you need, and how to use it

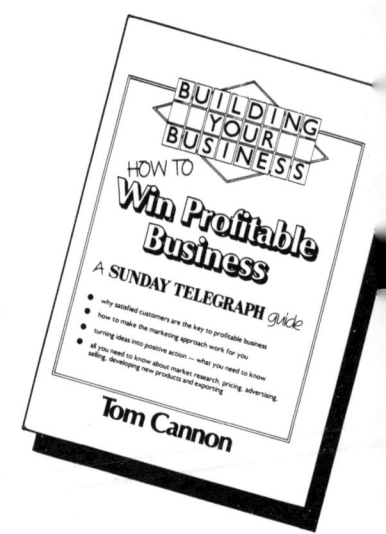

BUILDING YOUR BUSINESS

HOW TO **Win Profitable Business**

A SUNDAY TELEGRAPH guide

- why satisfied customers are the key to profitable business
- how to make the marketing approach work for you
- turning ideas into positive action — what you need to know
- all you need to know about market research, pricing, advertising, selling, developing new products and exporting

Tom Cannon

was your first problem.
going and growing.

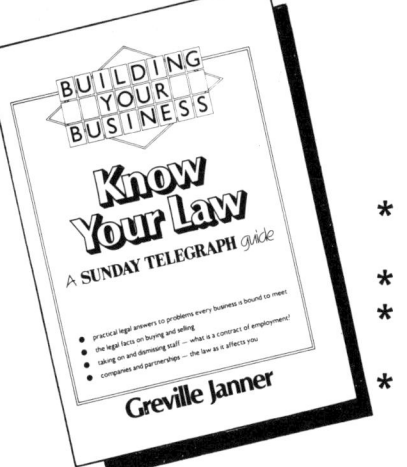

* practical legal answers to problems every business is bound to meet
* the legal facts on buying and selling
* taking on and dismissing staff — what is a contract of employment?
* companies and partnerships — the law as it affects you

Building Your Business books are available from your local bookseller. You can also order copies direct from Business Books, using the form below.

ORDER YOUR COPIES TODAY!

Please send me copies of the books ticked below, together with your invoice.

☐ Know Your Law   £5.95
☐ How to Manage Money   £5.95
☐ How to Win Profitable Business   £5.95

Name_____ Position_____

Company _____

Address _____

_____

POST TO: **Vivien James, Business Books, FREEPOST 5, London W1E 4QZ.** You do not need to stamp your envelope.

Business Books